Religions of the World

Series Editor: Ninian Smart

Religion in the Twenty-first Century

Mary Pat Fisher

Prentice Hall Inc., Upper Saddle River, NJ 07458

Published 1999 by Prentice Hall Inc.
A Division of Simon & Schuster
Upper Saddle River, New Jersey 07458

ISBN 0-13-690272-3

This book was designed and produced by Calmann & King Ltd, London

Editorial work by Melanie White and Damian Thompson
Pronunciation guide by Heather Gross
Design by Design Deluxe and Karen Stafford
Artworks by Sarah-Jayne Smith and Karen Stafford
Picture research by Peter Kent
Printed in China

Reviewers Mary Zeiss Stange, Skidmore College, New York; A. Joseph Everson, California Lutheran University; David Carlson, Franklin College, Indiana

Picture Credits

Cover Joseph Sohm, ChromoSohm Inc./Corbis; *page 17* © Vladimir Laitsev; *18* Sarah Thorley/Barnaby's Picture Library; *32* Mary Pat Fisher; *67* Peter Sanders; *83* Corbis-Bettmann/UPI; *86* Trygve Bolstad/Panos Pictures; *109* The Baha'i Information Office; *115* Mary Pat Fisher

Contents

7 sections

- 7 oral
presentations
in Groups

Foreword

Religions of the World

The informed citizen or student needs a good overall knowledge of our small but complicated world. Fifty years ago you might have neglected religions. Now, however, we are shrewder and can see that religions and ideologies not only form civilizations but directly influence international events. These brief books provide succinct, balanced, and informative guides to the major faiths and one volume also introduces the changing religious scene as we enter the new millennium.

Today we want not only to be informed, but to be stimulated by the life and beliefs of the diverse and often complex religions of today's world. These insightful and accessible introductions allow you to explore the riches of each tradition—to understand its history, its beliefs and practices, and also to grasp its influence upon the modern world. The books have been written by a team of excellent and, on the whole, younger scholars who represent a new generation of writers in the field of religious studies. While aware of the political and historical influences of religion these authors aim to present the religion's spiritual side in a fresh and interesting way. So whether you are interested simply in descriptive knowledge of a faith, or in exploring its spiritual message, you will find these introductions invaluable.

The emphasis in these books is on the modern period, because every religious tradition has transformed itself in the face of the traumatic experiences of the last two hundred years or more. Colonialism, industrialization, nationalism, revivals of religion, new religions, world wars, revolutions, and social transformations have not left faith unaffected and have drawn on religious and anti-religious forces to reshape our world. Modern technology in the last 25 years—from the Boeing 747 to the world wide web—has made our globe seem a much smaller place. Even the moon's magic has been captured by technology.

We meet in these books people of the modern period as a sample of the many changes over the last few centuries. At the same time, each book provides a valuable insight into the different dimensions of the religion: its teachings, narratives, organizations, rituals, and experiences. In touching on these features, each volume gives a rounded view of the tradition enabling you to understand what it means to belong to a particular faith. As the native American proverb has it: "Never judge a person without walking a mile in his moccasins."

To assist you further in your exploration, a number of useful reference aids are included. Each book contains a map, glossary, pronunciation guide, annotated reading list, and index. A selection of images provides examples of religious art, symbols, and contemporary practices. Focus boxes explore in more detail the relation between the faith and some aspect of the arts—whether painting, sculpture, architecture, literature, dance, or music.

I hope you will find these introductions enjoyable and illuminating. Brevity is supposed to be the soul of wit: it can also turn out to be what we need in the first instance in introducing cultural and spiritual themes.

Ninian Smart
Santa Barbara, 1998

Preface

At the dawn of the twenty-first century, we are living amidst a great global mixing of religious cultures. My own story is a case in point.

It begins in Louisiana, where I was raised in a Methodist Christian household. Jesus's message originally delivered in Palestine had taken seventeen centuries to reach American shores through European settlers. My mother's people came from Ireland during those early migrations, and I was named after the mother of Jesus. Our pastor was a kindly man who taught us the principles of Christian living by his own humble example. In addition to attending his worship services, I used to sit alone in the church, silently waiting to witness I knew not what. I also sat alone in a great magnolia tree, quietly happy, for hours at a time. Perhaps I was meditating, in a sense, but at the time I had no knowledge of inner spiritual practices or other ways of worship.

My first awareness of other branches of the world tree of religion was of Roman Catholicism. It seemed like a different world, though also based on the life and teachings of Jesus. My grandmother was a converted Catholic. When we visited her in Missouri, she delighted in taking me to a nearby convent and introducing me to the nuns and the relics of saints. Visiting the great cathedrals of Europe as a teenager, I was again awed by the holy mysteries of the Roman Catholic Church.

Like many Americans of that time, I nonetheless drifted away from religion, caught up in educational and material pursuits and in raising a family. Our family nonetheless celebrated the big Christian holidays, particularly Christmas, which has become a global holiday, partly because of its commercial exploitation.

When I turned thirty, my life took a major shift toward religion when I had a near-death experience. I was in a hospital, recovering from an operation, when a post-operative infection set in. No doctors were available; the busy nurses abandoned me. To fight against a raging fever, I tried to become very still so that my body could heal itself. In that stillness, I discovered that I was not alone in the room. It was filled with the presence of something or someone that I could not see. Its nature was absolute, unconditional love. The experience was so unspeakably beautiful that I never wanted to be separated from that presence. I prayed to it, "This body now belongs to You. Whether You choose to keep it alive or not is Your choice. But please always keep me with You; please allow me to serve You. But please don't take me away from my children."

From that time onward, I joined a growing surge of religious "seekers." I did not know that others were similarly searching for spiritual meaning and spiritual purpose, but by the 1980s there were many of us in the United States and Europe. My own search took me into a Lutheran Christian church, and from there, into studies with a variety of teachers from other religions whose roots reached around the world. In rural New England alone, I found and took spiritual instruction from native people of the Americas, from a Hasidic Jewish rabbi whose masters came from Central Europe, from American yoga teachers who had studied with Hindu masters in India, from American Buddhist teachers whose masters had come from Japan, from a Sufi master whose father was an Indian Muslim and mother an American and who had been raised in France and educated in England, from a German Roman Catholic monk who gives lectures around the world, from Russian Orthodox Christian monks, from Scotch mystics whose gardening community has become a global gathering place, and from a Taoist master from Korea. In the course of research for my textbook, *Living Religions*, I also lived in the homes and spiritual communities of followers of many new and old religious movements.

Finally, when my youngest child had left the nest, I met my ultimate teacher, Baba Virsa Singh, a great visionary of Sikh background living in India who communicates to people of all religions and all walks of life. I now live in his community fulltime, doing volunteer service. Under Babaji's inspiration, we celebrate the holidays of all faiths with great enthusiasm and learn sincerely to love all prophets.

As more people around the world are similarly becoming exposed to a multiplicity of religions, the need and opportunity arises for us to know more about each other. In this book, I have attempted to delineate processes which are now having an impact on all religions, both old and new, and to illustrate ways in which religions are evolving to meet the new challenges. Contrary to earlier expectations that religion would wither away in the face of science, logic, or materialism, we see that religion is very lively at the dawn of the twenty-first century. In previous millennia, religion played a central role in peoples' lives, and there are strong indications that religion is again coming to the fore as a major foundation for human life and thought.

To explore the complexities of religious expressions today, this book gathers perspectives from sociology, political analyses, psychology, and science, as well as the history and phenomenology of religions. It is therefore useful not only for studies of world religions but also for interdisciplinary courses, such as peace studies, future studies, and preparations for social service or health care. To benefit both from overall perspectives and in-depth analyses, it weaves together both approaches, with generalizations illustrated by specific examples. Chapter 1 examines modern and postmodern global processes now affecting all religions. Chapter 2 traces the original teachings and contemporary expressions of five major religions, plus indigenous spiritual traditions. Chapter 3 looks at new religious movements. Chapter 4 explores relationships between religions today, including manifestations of the interfaith movement.

The book has been appraised in great detail and improved according to the helpful suggestions of the reviewers listed on the imprint page.

For help in gathering materials, I am particularly grateful to G. S. Anand, Marcus Braybrooke, David Craig, Kitty Ferguson, Marianne Fisher, Virginia Hawkins, Chatsumarn Kabilsingh, Sarah Scott, and Madhuri Santanam Sondhi. My long-time and much appreciated editor, Melanie White of Calmann and King in London, has been extraordinarily helpful in pulling the material together.

My prayer is that this little book will deepen our understanding of and sensitivities to other people's points of view in our increasingly pluralistic world. May it also deepen our own links with ultimate reality, by whatever path we approach it.

Mary Pat Fisher
July 1998

<table>
<tr><td>Global
Processes</td><td>1</td></tr>
</table>

Global Processes | 1

What does religion look like at the dawn of the twenty-first century? Where is it going? To answer these questions is rather like the ancient Indian fable of the blind people trying to describe an elephant. Each grasps it in a different place and thus offers a different description. One takes hold of a leg and describes "elephant" as a pillar. Another takes hold of the trunk and declares that an elephant is like the branch of a tree.  One who touches the ear asserts that it is like a fan. The one who grabs the tail insists that an elephant is like a thick rope. One who comes against its side argues that an elephant is like a wall. The one who encounters the tusk says that the others are all wrong, for an elephant is like a spear.

Similarly, if people were to try to grasp and describe religion today from singular points of view, they would offer entirely different perspectives on the contemporary state of religion and different speculations about where it is heading. A person living in Sri Lanka or what was once called Yugoslavia might conclude that religion inevitably leads to deadly conflict between followers of various creeds. A person walking through downtown Las Vegas might decide that religion is irrelevant in contemporary life; ardent consumerism is of primary interest, and only money is considered to be of ultimate value. A person doing research in a scientific institution might determine that only self-deluded, ignorant people are following religions today; true answers about the nature of reality can be approached only through empirical methods. By contrast, a person involved in a liberal Jewish synagogue or a cooperative for the homeless run by Christian nuns might conclude that religion is very relevant to contemporary life and that it is becoming less patriarchal and more socially concerned. A woman kept in seclusion at home in Afghanistan might disagree, for her experience is that religion is becoming more socially restrictive, especially for women. And a person holding hands with Hindus, Muslims, Christians, Buddhists, Jews, Sikhs, and people of native religions at an interfaith conference in Chicago might conclude that the old hard boundaries between religions are softening and that a new era of interfaith cooperation is dawning.

Stepping back to survey the world as a whole, we can see all these divergent trends in operation today, and we might reasonably speculate that many of them will continue in the future. Yet at the same time, I have sought to identify common processes that are now affecting all religions. These often contradictory factors—**modernization**, **globalization**, exclusivism, humanism, and postmodernity—are likely to be influential in molding religion in general in the early twenty-first century.

Modernization

Religion does not exist in a vacuum. It is embedded in societies. In recent centuries, life in local communities has rapidly become more complex, partly through processes associated with modernization. Since the beginning of the sixteenth century, Western Europe and then North America have been the leaders in modernization, but from imitation triggered by economic pressures, all regions have been drawn into this accelerating trend. In the process, every social structure has been transformed. What are the typical features of this sea-change? A population shift from the countryside to the cities is triggered by technological progress in the manufacture or production of commodities. Naturally, at the same time, agricultural work that is in tune with the seasons gives way to industrial labor. Political control tends to become centralized in the nation-state, rather than being dispersed in the regions. At the same time, there may be a concentration of power in the hands of an educated and occupationally specialized middle class. On a broader level, new relationships are formed between individuals and bureaucracies, while traditional cultural and family-oriented patterns are often diluted. This in turn leads to new ways of behaving and thinking about the world. These are enormous changes. In 1900 only 9 percent of the world's population lived in cities. By the beginning of the twenty-first century, over 50 percent of the population are living in urban areas.

Religion once played a central role in society, and some argue that modernization has contributed to its relegation to a more separate, specialized role. In the modern nation-state, politics, economics, social policy, and education are no longer predominantly informed by religious values. In the United States, for example, religion and state are kept constitutionally separate, so as to guarantee the rights of believers from diverse faiths. Individual choice, sometimes balanced by the needs of the majority, tends to take precedence over traditional ways and traditional authorities. Religious beliefs are considered subjective choices rather than absolute laws, and material success is the object of many people's striving. Some argue that, divorced from religion, modern industrialized cultures tend to be ambivalent about ethical questions; they also contend that there is increased pressure, encouraged by advertising, to consume beyond one's basic needs, and a breakdown of traditional norms, such as respect for elders and family structures.

One school of thought even argues that modernization increases the gap between rich and poor. Capitalism, it is claimed, accentuates both wealth and poverty and increases the likelihood of unemployment, fear of the future, and feelings of alienation. All this is not to deny the positive features of modern urban existence—its vibrant pluralism, cultural life, and economic advantages for many; but it is argued by some that much has been lost in the spiritual sphere.

Globalization

A related process is the "shrinking" of the globe and the increasing interlinking of people from all corners of the planet. Geographic distances between cultures have been rendered less significant as a result of improved travel and communications technologies. All parts of the planet are also increasingly linked in the global economy, as capital flows internationally with lightning speed in search of favorable exchange rates, and multinational companies fan out in search of cheaper labor. These global corporations—most of which do more than half of their business abroad—now control fully one-third of the world's money and handle 70 percent of its trade. Fewer village farmers plant crops or artisans create their wares for local consumption alone. In most regions, they have been drawn into an unprecedented international system of free trade and monetary values.

The Spread of Religions

At the same time, globalization has led to an unprecedented mixing of cultures. For one thing, large-scale migrations of people have taken place across national boundaries. For several centuries, increasing numbers of people have been leaving their homelands to settle elsewhere, either seeking financial improvement or fleeing from oppression and violence, as old structures fall apart and people fight to establish new ones.

An estimated two million Muslims have migrated to the United States from Eastern Europe, the Middle East, Africa, Asia, and the Caribbean, and there are now fifty Muslim mosques in the city of Chicago alone. Toronto is now home to approximately 100,000 Sikhs from India. Many of them had left their homeland, the state of Punjab, after over four million Sikhs were displaced by the political partition of India in 1947 between Hindus and Muslims. Wherever Sikhs became immigrants—from Kenya and Singapore to England and Canada—they mingled with the local population, but also tried to maintain signs of their own cultural heritage. They built *gurdwaras* (Sikh temples) and many continued to wear their traditional dress. Generations after their emigration, many still feel politically as well as religiously linked to the Sikhs who have remained in Indian Punjab.

In addition to mass population shifts, religions have been dispersed by missionary activities. Christian missionaries have long fanned out around the world to serve the needy and preach the gospel of Jesus. But now that most lands have been reached by Christianity, giving it the greatest number of followers of any religion, Christian denominations are competing with each other for the conversion of souls to their particular version of the faith. As soon as communist control of the former Soviet Union fell apart in the early 1990s, planeloads of Protestant Christian evangelists began arriving in Russia to distribute Bibles, to the dismay of Russian Orthodox Christian clerics who felt that Russia was historically their territory.

Charismatic traveling religious teachers, such as Paramahansa Yogananda of the Self-Realization Fellowship (see pages 41–3) and A.C. Bhaktivedanta Swami Prabhupada of the Hare Krishna movement (see pages 75–6) have also been successful in recruiting converts in other countries. Both teachers journeyed from India to the United States to bring Hindu beliefs and practices to the attention of Westerners. In the 1970s Swami Prabhupada formed an international network of Krishna devotees called ISKCON, or International Society for Krishna Consciousness, whose followers took to the shopping malls, parking lots, and airports of America, dressed in Indian clothing, distributing classic Hindu scriptures in translation and enlisting new members.

An immediate impact of globalization is that religious cultures are no longer isolated from each other. No longer do people live out their lives under the influence of a single belief system. Fleeing oppression from China, Tibetan Buddhist monks who previously lived insular lives in high mountain monasteries are now scattered around the world; factory workers in New Mexico now have Tibetan monks as neighbors. South America, until recently solidly Roman Catholic, is now experiencing ardent proselytizing by Protestant missionaries. The Muslim call to prayer is now broadcast from the towers of mosques in London, and elaborate Hindu temples are being constructed across the English landscape. In the United States, Christian churches and seminaries have been converted to centers for Hindu and Buddhist meditation, and sweat lodges for spiritual purification in the Native American tradition are being constructed in people's backyards.

Acceleration of the processes by which religions spread geographically has led to what Professor Diana Eck, chair of the Pluralism Project at Harvard University, calls "the new geo-religious reality." Eck has documented many contemporary examples of the newly variegated religious landscape of the planet, including an extensive CD-ROM project depicting the pluralism of religions in the United States. She concludes,

> It is precisely the interpenetration and proximity of ancient
> civilizations and cultures that is the hallmark of the late
> twentieth century. This is the new geo-religious reality. The
> map of the world in which we now live cannot be color-coded
> as to its Christian, Muslim, Hindu identity; each part of the
> world is marbled with the colors and textures of the whole.[1]

The Global Village

Even without traveling, people living in different parts of the planet can now readily communicate with each other by telephone, fax, and computer networks. At the end of the twentieth century, it has become common to speak of the **global village**—the planet as a single community linked by telecommunications. International computer connections were a new phenomenon in 1990; within a few years, millions of people could engage in computer conversations on an ever-expanding array of topics, forming new "virtual communities" in cyberspace that transcend traditional geographical communities.

All communication technologies are expanding. Satellites orbiting the earth beam television programs far from their countries of origin. International trade in books is increasing and translations are proliferating. The classic Taoist scripture, the *Tao te Ching*, was little known beyond East Asia until the twentieth century. But in recent decades it has been translated into more languages than any book except the Bible. Newsletters, audiotapes, and videotapes are also being extensively used to carry messages from one location to distant regions.

By such means, new trends are now spreading very rapidly. In the past, it took ten centuries from the lifetime of the Buddha for his teachings to spread from his native India to Japan. By contrast, American "mind–body" doctor Deepak Chopra published *The Seven Laws of Spiritual Success* in 1994, and within three years it had been translated into thirty languages and distributed round the world. Chopra also propagated his ideas through other books, cassette tapes, and seminars, and received over a hundred letters every day from people in dozens of countries. He developed a newsletter and local study groups to keep them actively involved in his "spiritual movement directed toward global consciousness," with the hope of reaching "a critical mass of successful people that could transform life on Planet Earth."[2] At present, there are countless groups, religious and otherwise, new and old, that are racing to recruit a critical number of followers in order to accomplish their own planetary mission.

The virtual terrain of computer networks has also transcended the former geographical bases of religions. Computer links make it possible for new religious organizations to create and maintain contact with farflung communities of believers without the need to establish expensive buildings, clerical bureaucracies, or printing houses. Relatively new evangelical and Pentecostal Christian churches have very effectively used electronic technologies to propagate their message. So has the technologically literate Hindu **diaspora** (followers living away from their traditional lands). The Hinduism Forum of America Online is an electronic bulletin board with 5,000 postings, including scriptures, pictures of deities, discussion of vegetarian lifestyles, and answers to common questions about Hinduism. The Internet website of guru Sri Karunamayi supplies her history, her talks about character-building, Hindu virtues, and meditation, and her photos—including pictures of her feet for worshipers—plus calendars and maps of her world travels.

Similarly, a venerable Buddhist temple near Hiroshima has created a virtual cemetery where one can dedicate a virtual "tomb" for the dear departed, and thereafter "visit" the site from any location in order to remember and to pray. Monks at the temple also pray daily for the departed, whose memories rest in the temple's twenty computers. A Shinto shrine in Tokyo offers virtual pilgrimages to its sacred precincts, in which

ART FOCUS

Global Realization in Visionary Art

As SPIRITUAL CULTURES MIX, their intertwining may be reflected spontaneously in art forms as well as in more formal religious observances. A further artistic feature of our times is the flourishing of visionary art which exists outside of, yet may still refer to, specific institutionalized religions. Visionary art springs from inner truths which are themselves considered the mystical core of the various religions.

These features are exemplified in the work and ideals of the contemporary Russian visionary artists Vladimir Laitsev and Natalia Kravtchenko. Like many Russians today, they are influenced by Orthodox Christianity but are also very sympathetic toward the religious wisdom of India and mystical experiences of nature. They explain:

There are as if two realities, and which one is real? There is the routine life: You may have a car, a house, a good office, and thus it goes on for years. And you have tension. The other reality—the life of childhood, the life of natural communication with nature—is absolutely forgotten. Once you go outside in the mountains or the desert, or in some place where you can touch your roots again, you recollect everything. People tell us that this is not real life. But how is it possible to say that this wind, this sound of the river, is not real life?

Once Vladimir painted a face with light, with compassion, an image which appears from nature, from mountains, from heavens. We call it Pralaya. [In Hindu cosmology] there are two cosmic processes: emanation and dissolution, or Pralaya. Pralaya means when all the cosmos comes to rest, with its energy accumulated. It is not a final end. After millions of years, the universe appears again, with life, with trees, with rivers. It is a returning to the source, to the beginning, to the origin. It must be happy for beings, after long traveling, perhaps billions of years, to return to their source and be together.

As human beings, we have a very short lifespan, perhaps one hundred years maximum. How can we understand and feel Pralaya, which is a process of billions of years? But when it happens in our lives that we have knowledge about this, it means that we are not separate from this process.

We feel this is not only a matter of imagination. In the Vedic [ancient Indian] hymns, we found that everything was poetically glorified. There are hymns dedicated to rivers, mountains, rocks, stars, heavens, clouds. Everything is like one life. The human being is not separate from this life. He is part of this universe. It is inside him and outside him.

Vladimir Laitsev, Pralaya, *1996. Dry pastel.*

These understandings came from intuition, from intuitive knowledge. Sometimes what we have written in our poetry or expressed in our paintings, we later find in real life or in scriptures. We are sometimes shocked: "How did this image come to us if we did not know, if we never read the Hindu scriptures in Russia?"

What we find in the icon painting tradition of Orthodox Christianity is also very important. Before making any image, the monk usually is undergoing a certain spiritual process. He is not taking any food for a week, or perhaps just limited food. He is praying. So he is responsible for his image, for what he is creating. Some icon paintings are done with gold background, so they give light from within. This means that the light is more important than the image. In our paintings, also, we try to express this light which we feel.

Vladimir Laitsev and Natalia Kravtchenko,
interviewed December 11, 1997.

believers can "walk" through the grounds, offer devotions, and choose traditional paper flowers that foretell the future—all while sitting miles away at a computer.

The Internet provides anyone with access to a computer—chiefly available to those in the West—with a global audience. Many religious organizations, both large and small, have their own website on the Internet and use it to propagate their message globally. The Vatican set up its own website in 1995 and was immediately flooded with responses to its "E-mail the Pope" feature. Now the site contains press releases from the Vatican, details of the Pope's schedule, and writings of the Pope translated into six languages, and can simultaneously answer thousands of requests for information from around the globe. Pope John Paul II enthusiastically welcomed computer telecommunications as an opportunity for what he called "the new evangelization."[3]

At a gurdwara in Coventry, England, immigrant and second-generation Sikhs maintain their traditional dress and patterns of devotion from India. Here reverence is being paid to the scripture, the Guru Granth Sahib (center).

New religious groups can also be found in abundance on the "Net." For instance, Neo-pagans meet in cyberspace to hold virtual ceremonies, complete with computer graphics of altars, flames, and offerings.

One can also find on the Internet a number of interfaith directories to religious organizations who are interested in mutual understanding across sectarian boundaries. Derbyshire, in England, is the somewhat unlikely home to a very diverse religious community, including not only various Christian churches but also twenty Buddhist centers, thirty-nine Hindu temples, a Jain temple, fifteen Jewish synagogues, 153 Muslim mosques, and sixty-five Sikh *gurdwaras*. This on-the-ground local diversity is reflected in the University of Derby's MultiFaithNet computerized resources, which offer information about interfaith initiatives, aids to prayer and meditation such as sacred texts, music, and films from all religions, a multifaith religious art "gallery," discussion groups, video-conferences, on-line publications, a question-and-answer "corner" about religions other than Christianity, and connection to university classes and seminars in Religious Studies.

Exclusivism

While modern technologies are increasing awareness of the many varieties of religions and economic pressures are tending to create a transnational pool of potential believers, a contrary trend is also becoming more prevalent—and more noticeable, because it seems out of step with modernization and globalization. Some religious groups are trying to close their boundaries and limit their members' contact with other religions or forcibly to assert their singular claim to truth. This exclusivism can be seen as a reaction to the culture shocks of modernization and globalization suffered by previously isolated local cultures. Some people from traditional religious cultures find the sudden exposure to these unfamiliar modes of life distressing and dangerous for the health of society. They seek a return to a way of life in which the individual's self-interest is subsumed to the interests of the group as a whole and in which standards of conduct are strictly enforced.

Religions have traditionally set standards for acceptable behavior. Orthodox Judaism provided a very precise set of laws governing many aspects of daily life. Christianity, as expressed in the New Testament, encouraged the ethics of love. Islam developed social laws based on scripture and institutionalized customs, often derived from the exemplary life of the Prophet Muhammad. Buddha prescribed many imperatives for ending suffering, such as right livelihood and right thought. Traditional Hindus have observed the Code of Manu, compiled by 100 C.E., emphasizing social duties and the sacrifice of individual desires for the sake of order in society. In the Hindu scripture *Bhagavad Gita*, the god Krishna spoke of

> A person who has given up all desires for sense gratification, who lives free from desires, who has given up all sense of proprietorship and is devoid of false ego—he alone can attain real peace.[4]

By contrast, what are the values instilled by the modern capitalist system, when untempered by a sense of social responsibility? The system was initially promoted with the ideal of human progress, but emphasis has tended to shift away from humans to money itself. Roman Catholic Pope Paul VI, in his encyclical "On the Development of Peoples," described the basic laws of the free market economy that is sweeping the world as these:

1. Its key motive is profit: Profit for profit's sake.
2. Its supreme law is competition: Survival of the fittest. The big fish gobble up the small fish.
3. The right to the means of production is absolute: This right is not relative. It has no limits. It has no social obligation.[5]

Reactionary "Fundamentalism"

As people are turning away from older spiritual values through the influence of many factors, such as modernization and exposure to other cultures, the local response has in some cases been reactionary. There is a strong desire to shield the young from "harmful" outside influences and to resurrect loyalty to traditional ways and firmness of religious belief. This agenda is often labeled **fundamentalism**, for its proponents believe their mission is to restore the authenticity of their particular faith. However, this label is problematic, for "fundamentalism" is often selective and determined by subjective interpretation rather than based on the essence of the ancient enlightened teachings. The Project on Religion and Human Rights, in its international study of "fundamentalism," reports that in general,

Fundamentalists are not anti-scientific or anti-rational (at least in their own view) and certainly not anti-technological; not declining in influence; not always militant; and not always poor or uneducated. What they *are* is reactive against many aspects of modern life, e.g., its pluralism, consumerism, materialism, and stress on the equality of men and women. Fundamentalists selectively choose certain normative "fundamentals" that define their faith and lives, while they oppose any spiritualization of teachings or metaphoric interpretations of sacred texts. Such an approach makes them exclusivist and separatist. They are also absolutist. They have no room for ambiguity or relativism, which tends to make them authoritarian. In ethics they are uniformly anti-permissive, particularly in matters of sexuality and of the role of women in society.[6]

Thus the Taliban, who in the late 1990s have been trying to establish military and political control of Afghanistan, instituted what they considered a return to traditional Islam in whatever territories they occupied. The Muslim teacher leading the Taliban movement sent his students forth, not only to quash fighting between rival factions, but also to transform Afghanistan into a "pure" Islamic state of unprecedented rigidity. So, for example, they ordered women to stay off the streets unless they were clad head-to-foot in traditional clothes. Women were forbidden to work outside the home unless their workplaces could be reorganized to prevent their contact with men. All families were ordered to paint their windows black so that no passersby could see the women inside. All men were ordered to grow beards. Thieves were punished publicly by amputation of their hands.

There is, however, no general agreement about how an Islamic culture should be constituted. Muslim scholars have criticized the Taliban punishments as misunderstanding of *shariah*, Muslim law. In neighboring Iran, which had portrayed itself as a global model for revolutionary Islam, religious strictures are being eased, women are being appointed to high government posts, and intellectuals are freely discussing the degree to which Muslim law should be applied to a society.

Political Use of Religious Identity

In their reaction to contemporary pressures, people often seek to establish a new Utopian vision or, more commonly, to restore an idealized past, whether or not it ever existed in fact. This longing may be exploited politically.

In India, the RSS (Rashtriya Svayamsevak Sangh) arose early in the twentieth century, promoting Hindu cultural renewal and espousing the rebirth of an ancient Hindu Nation. In fact, the word "Hindu" does not appear in any Indian scriptures, nor is there one religion than can accurately be called "Hinduism." Religious paths have long been so diverse and deities so numerous in India that the subcontinent's ancient scriptures, the Rig Vedas, declare that "Truth is one; sages call it by various names." Nevertheless, the RSS has become a powerful movement, with branches in tens of thousands of Indian villages. Men gather there for group games, training in martial arts, music, lectures, and prayers supporting the "Hindu Nation."

Such reactionary sympathies of the populace are easily co-opted for political gain by power-seeking politicians. The Bharatiya Janata Party, the political manifestation of the RSS, has garnered great public support in India by portraying Hindus as the rightful inhabitants of the country, and Muslims and Christians as foreign interlopers. The BJP has thus agitated to topple Muslim mosques which had been built by the Mughal rulers over older temples to Hindu deities. In 1992 a huge mob was incited to destroy a Muslim mosque in Ayodhya, said to have been built over an ancient temple marking the birthplace of Lord Ram, the legendary perfect ruler. They were told by their political leaders that this violent act would be a step toward restoring Hindu virtues in society. In 1998, the BJP government won internal political support by conducting nuclear tests as a potent symbol of nationalistic strength. The head of the religious affiliate of the RSS, the Vishva Hindu Parishad ("World Hindu Society"), proposed that a temple should be built over the test site to celebrate the boosting of "the self-respect of the people of the country" by the nuclear tests.[7]

When several weeks later, Muslim Pakistan retaliated by conducting its own nuclear tests, millions of Pakistanis at once gathered to offer thanksgiving and prayers for Islamic unity. The prayer leader in Lahore's major mosque told the congregation that the nuclear explosions were "a great achievement for the entire Muslim world." He and other Muslim leaders deflected fears about the potentially crippling effects of international economic sanctions by calling for austerity measures as an adoption of an "Islamic way of life."[8]

In the politicization of religious "fundamentalism" a common strategy is to portray one's own group as insiders and others as outsiders. For instance, many Muslims have been misled into thinking that only Muslims are *mu'min* (believers), and that non-Muslims are *kafir* (non-believers). This is a convenient distinction for politicians who want to incite the people to group allegiance and hatred of others. However, the true meaning of these words does not refer to specific religious beliefs. *Kafir* means "one who hides truth"; *mu'min* means "one who disseminates truth."

Group Identification

Exclusivism often takes its energy from people's desire for group support to withstand threats to their way of life. Distinctive dress and separate schools may be emphasized to create a sense of group identification and to defend one's culture from outside influences. This exclusivism can change the nature of relationships with people from other groups. From the fifteenth to the eighteenth century, the Sikh **Gurus** taught the oneness of religion and compiled a scripture containing the devotional hymns of Hindu and Muslim saints as well as those of Sikh Gurus. Even while being attacked by Muslim rulers, the Sikh Gurus maintained friendly relationships with Muslims. The reputation of the Sikhs was so noble that Hindu families considered it an honor to have their sons become Sikhs. However, in the late nineteenth century, Sikh scholars reacted defensively to the presence of Christian missionaries in India, and then to the popularity of a Hindu reform movement. They began to assert that Sikhism was not an offshoot of Hinduism, as foreign scholars had often claimed, but rather an entirely distinct religion with its own independent history and revelation. To emphasize their separateness, the reactionaries pressed for the revitalization of the outer symbols of their religious identity—long hair to be bound in a turban, a comb for keeping it neat, a bracelet to remind one of commitment to the faith, special underwear that could be worn as clothing in an emergency if one were called on to fight, and a small sword to be worn at all times. These symbols had been given to the community by the Tenth Sikh Guru, Guru Gobind Singh, to turn his oppressed and demoralized people into staunch defenders of people of all faiths from religious tyranny. He ordered his followers to dress distinctively so that they could not hide from their duty to uphold justice. The articles of dress were instead used politically during the twentieth century as symbols of political separation.

Racism

Religious exclusivism may have racist as well as political overtones. While not a new phenomenon, hate crimes and desecration and destruction of religious places seem to be on the rise around the world, as people are at times led to blame their frustrations and fears in the face of the uncertainties and changes of modern life on other religious groups.

The Christian Identity Movement in the United States has portrayed threats to the social status quo as being led internationally by a Jewish conspiracy. This movement has grown since the 1970s and has influenced the political far right and groups such as the Ku Klux Klan, the White Aryan Resistance, and the American Nazi Party. In its version of conservative Protestantism, violence is justified by the belief that we are experiencing the prophesied "tribulation" at the end of human history, and believers must defend themselves from the "Antichrist."

Racial distinctions, underwritten by religion, have led to terrible acts of violence in former Yugoslavia at the end of the twentieth century. Some observers feel that religious differences between Orthodox Christians, Roman Catholics, and Muslims living in the area became the focus of old ethnic hatreds which had merely been suppressed under communist rule and were revealed once that system fell. Others argue that these religions had coexisted for 500 years, but that religion and ethnicity were used as tools to mobilize people politically when competition for democratic power was unleashed.

Humanism and Scientific Inquiry

At the same time that considerable tension is building between religious pluralism and religious exclusivism, another global process is the questioning or rejection of religion itself. At the turn of the century, an estimated 20 percent of the world's people do not identify themselves with any religion. Some are involved in material pursuits, more interested in the here and now rather than in promises of eternity. Some have become disillusioned with what they see as the hypocrisy, self-interest, and lack of spirituality in religious institutions. Others have wondered about the nature of reality and the meaning of existence but have come to the conclusion that there is no scientific evidence of any transcendent power behind the scenes shaping human events. Even religious followers have been challenged to develop new understandings of their faith in the light of modern research into the human and cultural dimensions of their prophets and scriptures.

The nineteenth-century German philosopher Nietzsche (1844–1900) rebelled against the narrow version of Christianity within which he had been raised. He attacked institutionalized religion as a "curse," an attempt to shield people from fear of the unknown, an explanation of reality that has been displaced by the ascent of science. Karl Marx (1818–83), whose writings have been especially influential in shaping the history of the twentieth century, concluded that religion is a human creation, an opiate-like fantasy whose purpose is to keep people numbly contented despite oppression and injustice in society. Several generations of children in the large territories under communist control were therefore trained in "scientific **atheism**." In the erstwhile Soviet Union, scientists were highly valued, while religious practices and places were outlawed or strictly circumscribed.

Humanism is a related intellectual movement of the modern age. It emphasizes human ethics rather than supernatural matters. It has its roots not only in Marxism but also in thousands of years of human thought from ancient China and India (where Buddhists and Jains observe non-theistic philosophies), through classical Greece and Rome, to the Enlightenment and the scientific revolution in Europe. The Humanist Manifesto of 1973, signed by thousands of intellectuals, asserted:

> We can discover no divine purpose or providence for the
> human species. No deity will save us; we must save ourselves.
> Promises of immortal salvation or fear of eternal damnation
> are both illusory and harmful. They distract humans from
> present concerns, from self-actualization, and from rectifying
> social injustices. . . . Critical intelligence, infused by a sense
> of human caring, is the best method that humanity has for
> resolving problems.[9]

Rational human thought has been a cornerstone of the modern period. Even sacred scriptures, regarded with awe by the faithful as divine or enlightened revelations, have been boldly subjected to rational inquiry by twentieth-century **textual criticism**. Scholars point to many difficulties in reconstructing the originals of texts such as the New Testament Bible, and cast doubt on the claims that holy books are unerringly true. Since 1985 a group of scholars called the Jesus Seminar has been meeting to debate the authenticity of the sayings attributed to Jesus in the New Testament. They have concluded that many words said to have been uttered by Jesus were probably later formulations by the community of believers in their efforts to develop the Christian faith. This conclusion is radically different from the feeling of other contemporary Christians that the Bible is infallible and literally true. A compromise is evolving between these two extremes of bold skepticism and absolute belief: Some people now regard scriptures as documents whose original forms and meanings may not be fully accessible but whose interpretations are important today and whose articles of faith have their own validity.

Rigorous questioning has threatened even the pedestal of science itself. Its foundations lie in the seventeenth-century adoption of the scientific method for uncovering the truths of the universe. In this method, all propositions are to be subjected to testing and experimental proof by mathematical quantification. The fundamental assumptions behind this methodology include the belief that the universe operates according to predictable causes and effects, that its underlying patterns can be discovered through human research, that the universe is ordered by some single unifying scheme, and that the goal of science is the assertion of human power over nature, for human benefit.

Although these assumptions behind the scientific method have enabled great technological advances, the latest scientific research casts doubt on the validity of the assumptions themselves. **Quantum physics**, the study of the smallest particles of matter, has revealed that their existence and behavior is not based on our common-sense notions of cause and effect. In the late twentieth century, it has been proved that, for instance, the sub-atomic particles of which everything is composed never have simultaneously a specific position and a specific momentum. This fact makes no sense in terms of human logic.

Increasingly, twentieth-century thinkers are realizing that even if science answers the "how" questions, it cannot answer all the "why" questions. This remains the domain of what we understand as religion. As scientists are now studying chaos and complexity in the universe, they are developing a more humble opinion of human reason. Many are also now observing that the application of science without ethics has led to widespread destruction of the natural environment, and that technological advancement has not in itself brought happiness. Cutting-edge theoretical research is leading some scientists into lively dialogue, if not necessarily agreement, with people of religious faith. The discoveries of quantum physics are being compared to ancient Eastern sages' impressions of the nature of reality—depictions of vast universes after universes, with no beginning and no end. And the idea that an overarching intelligence permeates this endless space is not necessarily ruled out. Physicist Stephen Hawking asks, "What is it that breathes fire into the equations and makes a universe for them to describe?"[10]

Postmodernity

At the dawn of the twenty-first century, we are living in what some social scientists call the **postmodern** age. Modernization was characterized by urbanization, industrialization, and the optimistic idea that humankind would be liberated by technological progress. However, as suggested in this chapter, these processes have not led to entirely positive results. Environmental degradation, social violence, disparity between rich and poor, unemployment, and homelessness have still not been eradicated. Psychological distress is also prevalent. Over 24 million people in 107 countries are using the drug Prozac in order to live one day at a time by keeping at bay their depression and anxiety. The postmodern age, which is said to have begun in the 1960s and 1970s, is sometimes characterized by disillusionment and uncertainty about the future. This social and psychological disruption is often referred to as the **crisis of modernity**. The French scholar Alain de Benoist writes,

> Individuals feel uprooted by globalization. Feeling powerless, they erect walls, even if fragile and laughable. On the psychological level, individuals now feel dispossessed by overwhelming mechanisms, an increasingly fast pace and even heavier constraints—variables so numerous that they are no longer able to grasp where they stand. That this happens at a time when individuals are lonelier than ever, abandoned to themselves, when all great world-views have caved in, only intensifies this feeling of a nothingness. . . . Accordingly, globalization resembles a puzzle of splintered images. It provides no vision of the world.[11]

At this juncture in history, religious activities and groups are so varied that it is difficult to draw any general conclusions about what religion looks like or where it is heading. Reactions to the new uncertainties and speed of change range from exclusiveness and absolutism—erecting walls in an effort to create within them a more certain world—to a new openness in religious expression. This latter trend, which can be found within many religions, is sometimes called **postmodern spiri-tuality**. Professor David Ray Griffin discerns eight themes in this approach: (1) A person's identity is not isolated, but rather determined by relationships with family, society, and the environment. (2) Humans are not separate from the natural world or the divine reality. They can experience their essential oneness with nature. (3) Both the past and the future are of value and should be considered in the present. (4) The Divine and all living beings are co-creators of reality. (5) The sexes are equal, and metaphors for the Divine may be female or male. (6) Local communities, families, bioregions, and cultural regions should be the context for public policy, rather than individuals or nation-states. (7) Religion should be freed from the confines separating it from morality, politics, and economics, and separating one religion from another. Religions are seen as plural and equal. (8) The subordination of every-thing social, moral, religious, and aesthetic to materialistic economic policy is rejected.[12]

In the face of these many conflicting influences, what can be said about the shape of religion today and what will it look like in this new century? Having sampled the global social context, we now turn in the next chapter to look at some of the major religions themselves to see how some people are making them relevant to today's concerns, even though they first arose under entirely different historical circumstances.

Religious Traditions in the Modern World | 2

One prediction about the future of religion in general seems likely: Religious practices in the twenty-first century will for the most part retain their ancient roots. Some 77 percent of the world's population now belong to one of the previously established religions—Hinduism, Buddhism, Judaism, Christianity, Islam, Sikhism, Confucianism, Jainism, Taoism, or Shinto. (This figure also includes the belief-systems of traditional tribal cultures, or "indigenous spirituality.") Despite their long heritage, the world's religious traditions are dynamic, changing in response to new inspiration and new social situations. In this chapter, we will survey the traditional beliefs of **indigenous spirituality** as well as those of five major religions—Hinduism, Buddhism, Judaism, Christianity, and Islam. We will also take a close-up look at one contemporary manifestation of each, to illustrate how long-established religions are being redefined. The popularity of the new ways seems to lie not only in their initial vigor but also in their relevance to contemporary needs, such as environmental protection, racial reconciliation, women's rights, and solutions to the crisis of modernity. We will also look at other, often contrasting, directions in which each religion is currently evolving.

Indigenous Spiritual Traditions

Relatively little is known about the spiritual ways practiced by indigenous people who still live close to their land, such as certain natives of the Americas and small-scale societies in remote areas of the planet. For the most part, they are not literate cultures with written scriptures. Their religious frame of reference is their own environment, and wisdom is passed down from generation to generation orally. Additions to the traditions occur as new inspiration arises among the people or as they are influenced by other cultures.

It is thought that these ancient ways once existed everywhere. For the most part, they have been suppressed by, or fused with, the religions of cultures which are more politically powerful, such as Christianity or Hinduism. Yet in remote pockets on every continent—from sub-Arctic Canada to the Australian "outback"—some small-scale societies still attempt to practice their ancient ways.

These pockets are depleting in the face of globalization, so it is likely that these indigenous religions will be practiced in their time-honored form by even fewer people in the future. However, their influence is being felt in new ways and their teachings practiced in new forms by some people who were not born into traditional cultures. For several decades, traveling teachers from the ancient cultures of the Americas have been initiating followers in the cities of North America and Europe, and attempts to preserve the spiritual traditions of the remaining land-based cultures are increasing. A lively **Neo-pagan** movement has sprung up, seeking to revive and practice in contemporary ways the ancient pre-Christian indigenous traditions of Europe, by enthusiasts who have no direct connection with those traditions.

Traditional Beliefs and Practices

Despite their great variety, surviving indigenous cultures in general teach that all forms of life, all aspects of existence, are spiritually inter-related. The land, the people, the creatures, the weather, the unseen spirits, and the celestial bodies are interwoven strands forming the tapestry of life. Who weaves this tapestry? Some American tribal peoples say that it is Grandmother Spider, who continually spins the cosmic web. Around the globe, there are many names for this "great mysterious presence" which creates and interrelates all that is—such as the Great Spirit, Wakan Tanka, Kitche Manitou, the All-Powerful, the One Who Began the Forest, the Spirit of the Sky, the One Who is Never Fully Known. Unseen presences abound in all such cultures—spirits of the land, the water, the trees, the mountains, the ancestors, the elemental forces. In the visible world as well, everything is perceived as living and sentient. Trees and animals may communicate with humans, and even stones are filled with energy.

In the cosmic web, any movement on one strand sets the whole web shaking. Traditional indigenous peoples are therefore considered "environmentalists," for they say they feel a sacred relationship and responsibility to all of life. As Chief Seattle is supposed to have said in 1854,

This we know: The earth does not belong to man; man belongs
to the earth. This we know. All things are connected like the
blood which unites one family. All things are connected.
Whatever befalls the earth befalls the children of the earth.
Man did not weave the web of life; he is merely a strand in it.
Whatever he does to the web, he does to himself.[1]

How, then, does one live in sacred relationship with all life? From
childhood, the people are taught the origins of the cosmos, usually
through stories which have some specific reference to their own environment. The Turkic peoples of Siberia narrate the story of creation with
reference to Tuvinian mountain; in the Amazon, the rain forest is the origin of the cosmos. From these cosmologies spring more songs, stories,
and dramas about the beings who people the cosmos and whose power
should be respected. The reenacting of these stories is part of the fabric
of life, and the people continually offer their reverence to the many
beings to whom they are related. The influence of certain unseen beings
may be malevolent, so one has to be careful as well as reverent. Before
cutting down a plant or killing an animal, an indigenous person may
offer apologies and gratitude for its life. The behaviors and speech of
birds may be carefully observed, for they are thought to be messengers
from the spirit world. The spirits within huge old trees are especially
revered around the world. Even in societies which have otherwise converted to one of the world's major religions, there are often signs of worship around ancient trees, such as offerings of food and flowers, and bits
of cloth tied to branches with prayers for the sick.

Although indigenous spirituality is said to permeate individuals'
everyday lives, it is also formalized in rituals and specialized sacred roles.
In small-scale cultures there may be priests and priestesses or costumed
members of secret societies who conduct group worship ceremonies to
mark the turn of the seasons, celestial events, and rites of passage such
as birth, puberty, marriage, and death. In most indigenous societies,
there are also men and women who have special spiritual abilities to
communicate with the spirit world and summon the help of unseen spirits. The Siberian term **shaman** is now used internationally to refer to
such visionaries and healers. They may use drums, rattles, or trance-
inducing herbs to facilitate their entry into an altered state of consciousness in which they can travel through the spirit world, bringing
back information and spiritual powers. They work in a state of ecstasy,
in which their own personality and thoughts are set aside so that the

Ancient trees, and the spirits that reside within them, are venerated by practitioners of different religions around the world. Food offerings, flowers, and strands of cloth are tied to the branches of a tree in New Delhi, India, with prayers for the sick.

unseen spiritual forces may work through them. Black Elk, a twentieth-century Native American shaman, explained,

> Of course it was not I who cured. It was the power from the outer world, and the visions and ceremonies had only made me like a hole through which the power could come to the

two-leggeds. If I thought that I was doing it myself, the hole would close up and no power could come through.[2]

Once thought mad by outsiders, shamans are now increasingly taken seriously and are sometimes called in by medical doctors as healers for indigenous people in medically incurable cases.

Many indigenous societies also have traditional methods by which individuals purify themselves inwardly and dedicate themselves to the good of the group. In the Americas, people gather in sweat lodges—small structures built over a pit into which heated stones are placed. As the temperature within the dark lodge becomes almost intolerably hot, people pray fervently for hours. When at last they emerge, they feel like babies emerging from the womb, humbled and cleansed of impurities. Such group processes give the people a continual feeling of connection to each other, to countless generations from the past, as well as to the yet-unborn generations to come.

During such intense experiences people may also have visions of the spirit world. These are carefully heeded as guidance or warnings for the individual or group. Dreams are also respected as meaningful prophecies. The Plains Indians' tradition of passing a sacred pipe around a circle, with each person holding and smoking it ritually, originated in a vision of White Buffalo Woman, who gave instructions about the sacred meaning and use of the pipe.

In indigenous societies, elders are usually highly respected, for it is they who remember the traditional songs and dramas, and whose wisdom is of great value to the community. Sharing is considered a major virtue, and in some cultures people sponsor lavish give-aways in which they redistribute all they have to others.

Indigenous Ways Today

Nostalgia for these nearly-lost traditions resurfaced in the twentieth century. This is not just a matter of sentimentality. Around the globe, indigenous people have seen their traditional ways of life destroyed as they have been forced off their lands by more powerful commercial interests, their sacred sites taken over for uses such as mining or tourism, and heavy pressure applied to convert to other religions, particularly Christianity. Reassertion of traditional ways and rights to their ancestral lands is thus a matter of cultural and economic survival. Although these small-scale societies have historically been isolated, they are now reaching out to each other for combined strength in resisting encroachments. They are forming regional, national, and global alliances and working with the United Nations to protect their rights and their cultures. They are often found on the frontline of resistance to nonsustainable uses of the land, for theirs are the few remaining pockets of land which can be protected from environmental destruction. In Panama, the Kuna Indians have managed to save and maintain a forest park and botanical preserve; the Kayapo Indians of Brazil were able to halt World Bank funding of a large-scale dam project; and the Cordillera Peoples' Alliance of the Philippines has stopped dams, blocked logging companies, and developed their own sustainable development projects.

To accomplish such goals, people from small-scale societies have increasingly adopted the technologies of the larger culture, using videotapes to document and protest against destruction of their forests, calling press conferences to block dam projects, publishing over 400 periodicals devoted to indigenous concerns, and **networking** with each other via computers. At the same time, they are challenged to maintain the integrity of their traditional nature-based principles. Ailton Krenak from the Brazilian Union of Indian Nations explains,

> We see it like this: It is as if we are all in a canoe traveling through time. If someone begins to make a fire in their part of the canoe, and another begins to pour water inside the canoe, or another begins to piss in the canoe, it will affect us all. And it is the responsibility of each person in the canoe to ensure that it is not destroyed. Our planet is like one big canoe traveling through time.[3]

Close-up: Neo-paganism

It is not just indigenous peoples who are renewing their commitment to their traditional principles. In the face of urban alienation from the natural environment, people from technologically advanced societies are seeking ways of re-establishing contact with the earth. Many are also searching for a more personal form of spirituality than what they see as the bureaucratic, authoritarian, and typically male-dominated structures and strictures of the major global religions. A popular postmodern answer to this search is to delve back into the nature-based religions of pre-Christian Europe—the presumed origins of the primarily white, middle-class people who are now practicing what is often called Neo-paganism.

The word **pagan** comes from the Latin word for "peasant," "countrydweller," "civilian." It was historically applied as a negative epithet to those who had not been converted to Judaism, Christianity, or Islam. Suppression of these non-converts by "witch-hunters" and the Roman Catholic Inquisition claimed millions of victims in Europe from 1350 to 1750. Christian churches were reportedly built over their ancient ritual sites, their folk festivals were given Christian significance, and their indigenous ways were gradually driven underground. Some say that pagan spirituality died out entirely; some say that it was kept alive in secret over the centuries by a few practitioners.

Margot Adler, a leading writer in the contemporary Neo-pagan movement and also New York bureau chief of National Public Radio, explains,

> Neopagans are searching among the archaic images of
> nature, among the ruins of traditions lost, in order to find,
> revive, and re-create the old polytheistic nature religions.
> The fascination with long dead pagan traditions is part of a
> search for cultural roots. Since most Neopagans are white,
> they often look toward Europe.[4]

Without written scriptures or centralized authority, Neo-pagans in Western urban cultures are evolving their own new ways with reference to the older nature-based traditions. Like the remaining indigenous peoples, Neo-pagans say they experience the natural world as alive, sentient, and sacred, permeated with invisible energies. The very rhythms of the cosmos are held sacred, so the cycles of sun and moon are honored and celebrated. Like the old agriculture societies from whom they are drawing inspiration, they celebrate the solstices, equinoxes, and full moons as important markers in the cosmic calendar. Geography is also assigned spiritual meaning, with north, east, south, and west forming a sacred circle in which each quadrant has its own significance. Life-cycle events such as giving birth and reaching the age of menopause are also ritually celebrated.

A distinctive feature of Neo-paganism as practiced in some contemporary circles is its interest in **magic**. Starhawk, a prominent neo-pagan writer and practitioner, defines magic as "the art of sensing and shaping the subtle, unseen forces that flow throughout the world, of awakening deeper levels of consciousness beyond the rational."[5] To this end, Neo-pagans use rituals in order to enter a state of communion with the unseen forces and to take their help in matters such as healing. Unlike members of small-scale indigenous societies, Neo-pagans did not learn such spiritual rituals from their ancestors. They are therefore freely creating new ones. They may gather in a natural place deemed to be especially powerful—or else in someone's urban apartment—form a circle, place candles and crystals, chant, sing, dance, drum, and invoke the unseen spirits. Someone may lead the group in a visualization process, an imaginary inward journey.

Psychologist Adrian Ivakkhiv explains the appeal of Neo-paganism as a "postmodern response to the disenchanted and depersonalized worldview of modernity":

This is the dilemma in which contemporary Euro-American society finds itself: as a culture, we have lost the sense of sacredness in our relationship with the world about us. The world we live in is a disenchanted one, made up of discrete, disconnected (or at least, not meaningfully connected) objects, amongst which we are free to do what we please; but we don't know what it is we should do or what our rightful place amidst it all is meant to be.[6]

Neo-pagan circles can thus be seen as trying to recreate the same sense of sacred meaning and connectedness with the cosmos as is claimed by indigenous religious cultures. Starhawk explains:

We invoke and become the Goddess and God linked to all that is. We experience union, ecstasy, openness. The limits of our perception, the fixation on a single note of the song, dissolve: We not only hear the music, but we dance the whirling, exhilarating, spiral dance of existence.[7]

The Neo-pagan movement is extremely diverse. Some Neo-pagans function in a serious manner; some are erotic; some are playful, imaginative, and eclectic, choosing favorite deities from any culture to worship; some are practical, using "destressing" rituals for contemporary malaise and spells for finding parking spaces in crowded cities.

Across the United States, at least sixty Neo-pagan festivals are held yearly at outdoor campsites, providing practitioners a surreal setting in which to transcend the usual social boundaries and take on any identity, wear any costume or bare their bodies, and create any "kinship" groups they choose. Such festivals may include ritual fires, storytelling, dancing, and workshops on subjects of interest such as divining the future through tarot cards, astrology, magic, Native American medicinal herbs, and drumming. Despite the atmosphere of freedom, participants also engage continually in self-analysis and discussions about which behaviors are acceptable and which are not.

The stigma attached to paganism and "witchcraft" centuries ago still lingers, and Neo-pagans are sometimes suspected of practicing devil worship or animal sacrifices. Though they emphatically deny these claims, many practitioners meet in relative secrecy to avoid disclosing their connection with the movement. But Sherrian Lea, an MIT student from Ohio who has "come out of the broom closet," explains that for her, as for many, Neo-paganism offers a sense of belonging to an ancestral tradition:

> My ancestors, or at least a subset of them, were Pagans who
> believed in elves and fairies, and lit fires on the solstices and
> equinoxes. I chose Paganism as opposed to the Eastern
> religions partly because I'm British and German. This is how
> I might have worshipped if I lived 2,000 years ago.[8]

"Hinduism"

Whereas indigenous peoples and Neo-pagans are attempting to reconstruct their past, India is home to a number of very ancient but overlapping religious ways. A diverse group of these practices and philosophies shares a common base in the ancient Vedic scriptures. They are commonly brought together under the umbrella term "Hinduism." The more correct, but less-known term for these practices is **Sanatana Dharma**, meaning the age-old way of directing all activities toward goodness in society and realization of the divine.

Many of the myriad ways of Sanatana Dharma can be traced to ancient civilizations in the Indian subcontinent dating from 2500 B.C.E. or earlier. Some are thought to be even older, having been brought to the subcontinent by Aryan migrants from southern Russia during the second millennium B.C.E., although this theory is now hotly disputed. And some are devotional practices that developed in the course of the seventh century C.E.

In contemporary India, devotees worship in many different ways, honor many different gods, and read a variety of scriptures. Through its followers who have emigrated to other lands, and the new religious movements it has spawned abroad, Sanatana Dharma is becoming increasingly visible on the world stage.

Traditional Beliefs and Practices

Despite the great diversity within Sanatana Dharma, all followers find common ground in certain major points. One is a foundation in the **Vedas**, ancient scriptures of unknown age, written down thousands of years ago. The Vedas are thought to be among the world's oldest holy texts. They contain **polytheistic** ("many deities") hymns of praise and supplication to various controlling forces in the cosmos personified as deities, and also the enlightened utterances of anonymous sages who had realized a singular eternal reality through meditation. These sages perceived the entire cosmos as emanating from a formless Being who continues to pervade every particle. As one of the sages explained,

> In the beginning there was Existence alone—One only, without a second. He, the One, thought to himself: Let me be many, let me grow forth. Thus out of himself he projected the universe, and having projected out of himself the universe, he entered into every being. All that is has its self in him alone. Of all things he is the subtle essence. He is the truth, He is the Self. And that, . . . That art thou.⁹

The sages realized that the soul, or *atma*, of each being is an emanation of the universal source, **Brahman**. Brahman could thus be discovered by looking within oneself. Once we realize our *atma* and its source, Brahman, we transcend worldly concerns and enter a realm of eternal peace.

Another major teaching of Sanatana Dharma is the **reincarnation** of the *atma*. It is said that at death, our body dies, but our *atma* adopts a new body and is reborn again. The process is like taking off old clothes and putting on new ones. The new incarnation and the experiences we face are a result of our *karma*—the effects of our past actions. If we have tormented others, we will be tormented in the next life. If we have behaved according to the eternal principles of *dharma*—righteousness and moral order—then our next incarnation will be very favourable. If we try very hard, lifetime after lifetime, to fully cleanse our *karma* and realize Brahman, then we may at last achieve liberation from reincarnation, freed from the miseries of the cycle of births, deaths, and rebirths.

Spiritual disciplines for clearing *karma* and realizing the *atma* and Brahman have been practiced since prehistoric times in India. Seals from the earliest of civilizations show a figure seated crosslegged in deep meditation. The practices are collectively known as **yoga**, which means "union"—union of the individual consciousness with the Infinite Consciousness. There are practices using the breath to attune a person to the timeless, practices with repetition of sacred words, practices with the subtle energies in the body, visual methods for concentrating the mind, and postures to calm the mind and allow energy to flow freely. The goal is *samadhi*—union of the individual awareness with the eternal and changeless.

Yogic practices are being revitalized in India, but worship is more popular than meditation. People can choose from millions of deities. Some love Lord Krishna, worshiped both as an adorable youth and as the enlightened cosmic Master. Others follow Lord Shiva, the ascetic creator and destroyer, the one by whose dance the whole cosmos is running, the one whose *samadhi* is so powerful that he can swallow the poison threatening to doom the world. Others revere some form of the Goddess, such as Durga Mata, who selflessly came to the aid of the gods when demons had overrun the world. Riding on a tiger, she slew all the demons and returned command of the world to the gods. There is Lord Ram, the exiled prince who fought an epic battle with the demon king and then governed the kingdom as the perfect ruler according to the principles of *dharma*. And there is Hanuman, the monkey king, who was so utterly devoted to Lord Ram that he could perform great feats of strength.

Stories of the gods and goddesses and their devotional worship form the bulk of popular religious practice among the people of India. The choice of a particular deity to worship is an intimately personal matter, and even within a single family, members may have particular devotion to different deities. All are ultimately understood as emanations of the same Unknowable One referred to in the ancient scriptures.

Worship goes on everywhere. Shopholders wave incense and pray before the deities in the shrine on their shop wall before starting business each day. Rare is the auto-rickshaw which is not adorned with deities' pictures. Temples to various deities are ubiquitous, and within them priests are available to conduct the ancient rituals with offerings of flowers, fruits, lights, and sacred fire ceremonies. Every home has its own area devoted to favorite deities, and family members daily worship before and care for their statues. The devotee longs for the direct experience of the divinethrough the medium of the statue.

This earnest devotion is known as **bhakti**. Many of India's great saints were practitioners of this way of love. In the sixteenth century there was Mirabai, a princess who ignored all worldly considerations for the sake of her love for Lord Krishna. Her passionate love for the deity and abandonment of her worldly roles infuriated her in-laws. They imprisoned her and even tried to poison her. Unconcerned, she danced before a statue of her lord. Her poetry is still revered as the epitome of *bhakti* worship. She sang,

> Do not lose hold of such a gracious Master!
> Offer thy body, mind and wealth
> To Him alone.
> Cherish His image in thy heart.
> Come, my companion, look at His face,
> Drink in the beauty with thine eyes.
> Act only to please Him, in every way.[10]

Festivals associated with the gods and goddesses are many, so the Indian calendar is marked by a great number of public holidays. People also make personal pilgrimages to sites mentioned in the stories of the deities or to remote places associated with them. They undergo great hardships to walk on foot to caves high in the mountains or to travel to holy rivers, so that their sins may be erased and their petitions to the divine may be accepted.

Some also worship a living teacher of the holy ways, a guru. Such a man or woman has supposedly achieved enlightenment and become imbued with the divine, and can supposedly show others the way to such realization and miraculously help and transform them by his or her spiritual power. In the ideal relationship, disciples faithfully surrender their own mind to be cleansed and remolded by the guru, without whose help one can never defeat the ego and its impediments to spiritual realization. But there are some who pose as gurus without the requisite enlightenment and spirit of selfless service, and thus mislead the people and abuse their faith.

Sanatana Dharma Today

Sanatana Dharma is as varied today as it has long been. Nineteenth-century Hindu reform movements such as Arya Samaj, which forbade idol worship and ritualism, still enjoy a following among Indian intellectuals.

Some 20 million Indians have become involved in the Swadhyaya movement, in which volunteers carry out village development projects based on principles found in the classic scriptures of Sanatana Dharma. Pilgrimage to sacred sites in the mountains is growing, and millions yearly undertake these difficult journeys. Certain gurus—such as the miracle-working Satya Sai Baba—have large followings. Everyday worship also proceeds as always.

"Hindu" spiritual identity is being fanned politically by the RSS (see Chapter 1). In contrast to the secularism of the 1949 Indian constitution, designed to defuse tensions between the majority Hindus and the large minority of Muslims, "Hindu-ness" is being proclaimed the cultural base of India, and Hindu extremists are developing an overtly political agenda. To strengthen their position, they are redefining Hinduism as a monolithic rather than variegated religion. Nationally, this exclusivist agenda is broadcast through ascetics working for the Vishva Hindu Parishad. They stage highly visible and highly publicized campaigns to unite the voters around their religious identification. Among these are massive caravans carrying symbols with universal appeal, such as water from the Ganges, the river held sacred by all Hindus. This appeal to Hindu unity and Hindu pride has been globalized; emigrants to other countries have joined resident Indians in building large new temples around the planet.

Not only has Sanatana Dharma spread through its diaspora; beginning in the nineteenth century, many self-proclaimed gurus left India to gather followers abroad. Foreigners were at first innocently ready to follow anyone wearing holy robes and proposing to lead them to enlightenment. At the end of the twentieth century, scandals such as financial exploitation and sexual abuses of their followers have marred the reputation of many Indian gurus teaching in the West and led to scepticism about gurus in general. Nevertheless, interest in Hindu beliefs and practices has caught the interest of non-Indians, and some of the organizations initiated by traveling gurus have become strong and widespread. Characteristically, they emphasize certain aspects of Sanatana Dharma—especially meditation and guru worship—to the near-exclusion of others.

Close-up: The Self-Realization Fellowship

One of the oldest and most respected transplanted Indian movements is the Self-Realization Fellowship. Its original guru was Paramahansa

Yogananda (1893–1952). His book, *The Autobiography of a Yogi* (1946), has become one of the classics of modern spirituality, and has been translated into eighteen languages. It recounts Yogananda's own spiritual journey, replete with visionary experiences, miraculous healings, and meetings with powerful spiritual figures in India. In it readers are also introduced to the philosophical principles of Sanatana Dharma— such as reincarnation, *karma*, and meditation for the purpose of spiritual realization. The author gives tempting glimpses of a meditation practice taught to him by his guru to raise and harmonize the body's spiritual energy with the energy of the cosmos. Yogananda claims that its practice is a shortcut to the goal of union with God, which otherwise, according to Hindu scriptures, may take a million years for a normally progressing soul. In addition to the promise of quick spiritual progress, Yogananda taught universal love and love for oneself, "because you are a child of God with divine potentials."[11]

Many twentieth-century Americans, with their individualism, interest in rapid progress, and new-found enthusiasm for Indian spirituality, adopted Yogananda's program for spiritual advancement and took initiation with him as their guru. He traveled across the continent, speaking before crowds of thousands, and built a temple and **ashram** (spiritual community) in California overlooking the Pacific Ocean. There Lord Krishna and Jesus Christ are worshiped side by side, for Yogananda taught that Jesus' teachings should be revered. Yogananda spoke of a new synthesis, combining Indian spirituality with American practicality.

After Yogananda's death, his work was carried on by his designated successors, who were American initiates, through the Self-Realization Fellowship which he had founded. His charisma still permeates the movement. It is also exceptionally well-organized and run by dedicated disciples, so its numbers are still growing. At the end of the twentieth century, several hundred thousand people are thought to have taken initiation into Kriya Yoga, more are engaged in home-study courses, and even more are exposed to Yogananda's ideas through an extensive publication program. Some 2,000 items based on his teachings, including audiotapes and videotapes, are published by a staff of fifty full-time workers and sold at cost. There are now ten "how-to-live" communities and temples run by the Self-Realization Fellowship in the United States, one in Germany, headquarters and social-welfare projects in India, and SRF centers and meditation groups in forty-four other countries.

Half a century after Yogananda's death, the stability of the movement he founded indicates that it may have lasting appeal in the twenty-first century. For its most dedicated Western practitioners, who live as ascetics in ashrams and are familiar with the spiritual teachings of classic Indian scriptures, there are clear links with the ancient traditions of Sanatana Dharma. Many others who have read Yogananda's words are not interested in a Hindu identity but in a personal search for the inner peace, joy, and spiritual transformation which Yogananda promised to those who would practice meditation. He affirmed the universality of divine love and spiritual assurance which many people are seeking today:

> The wisdom garnered by India, the eldest brother among the
> nations, is a heritage of all mankind. Vedic truth, as all
> truth, belongs to the Lord and not to India. . . . God is Love.
> . . . Every saint who has penetrated to the core of Reality has
> testified that a divine universal plan exists and that it is
> beautiful and full of joy. . . . [12]

Buddhism

Compared to Sanatana Dharma, Buddhism is a younger religion from India. Whereas the Vedic sages regarded union with supreme reality as the highest goal, Buddhism focuses instead on the reality of worldly suffering and on the skillful means for escaping from it. This was the realization of Gautama Buddha, who was born as a prince about 563 B.C.E. He left the life of luxury to become a wandering ascetic. His ardent goal was to find the way of freeing people from the suffering which he reportedly witnessed when traveling outside his palace—sickness, old age, sorrow, despair. After years of intense meditation, he at last achieved **enlightenment**, and then devoted the rest of his life to teaching others the means to liberation. His extensive teachings, compiled in many volumes and propagated by monks and nuns, spread throughout Asia from the third century B.C.E. to the thirteenth century C.E. During the twentieth century, they were embraced by many people in the West as well.

Traditional Beliefs and Practices

The Buddha's central teachings appeared in his very first sermon. Their essence is encapsulated in the Four Noble Truths:
1. Life inevitably involves suffering. It is imperfect and unsatisfactory.
2. Suffering is caused by our desires.

3. There is a state in which there is no suffering.
4. There is a way to achieve this state.

The Buddha proposed that the way to eliminate suffering is what he called the Eightfold Path: right understanding, right thought, right speech, right action, right livelihood, right effort, right mindfulness, and right meditation.

The Buddha looked at suffering in great detail and concluded that nothing is unchanging. We might want things to stay as they are, or to become as we want them to be. We want to grasp and control life, but we cannot, for it is naturally in constant flux. Sun will eventually be followed by rain; flowers will decay; the body will age. As Venerable Ajahn Sumedho, a present-day Buddhist teacher explains,

> Trying to arrange, control and manipulate conditions so as
> to always get what we want, always hear what we want to
> hear, always see what we want to see, so that we never have
> to experience unhappiness or despair, is a hopeless task.[13]

The only way to end suffering, then, is to detach ourself from this hopeless task. To do that, Buddha advised people thoroughly to understand the nature of the mind, to purify and retrain it, for the mind is subtle and treacherous. Meditation is the tool for quieting the mind so that it can clearly apprehend reality. The goal is enlightenment—inner awakening of direct perception of truth. Once the mind is under control, we can move through life freely and happily, no matter what our circumstances. The ultimate enlightened state of egolessness, quietness, and bliss is called *nirvana*.

Buddha also addressed the problem of *karma*. As in Sanatana Dharma, Buddhists aspire to be liberated from the endless process of births, deaths, and rebirths, which is fueled by our wrong thoughts, words, and actions. These, too, can be ended by the determined practice of meditation. "Pull yourself out as an elephant from the mud," the Buddha reportedly said.[14]

As the Buddha's teachings spread eastward through the centuries, two rather distinct groups developed. One has been called **Theravada**, the "Teaching of the Elders." It prevails today in Sri Lanka, Burma, Thailand, Cambodia, and Laos. Its practitioners feel that it is the purest form of Buddhism. The other group calls itself **Mahayana**, the "Greater Vehicle," for its adherents feel it is like a huge raft which can carry the masses better than the rather stark teachings of the Theravadans. Both practice the same teachings outlined above, and "take refuge" in the same three things: the Buddha, his teachings (the Dharma), and the community of disciples.

In Buddhism there is no mention of a creator god. The Buddha said that there are more things of which he had not spoken, but it is most useful for us to concentrate on the elimination of suffering. Although Buddhism is therefore **nontheistic**, Mahayana reveres Buddha-nature as a universal, eternal principle in the cosmos. Theravada regards the Buddha simply as a guide who left us invaluable teachings. Mahayana also holds that not only should we free ourself from suffering, we should also free others from suffering. The ideal is the **Boddhisatva**, a person who compassionately makes a strenuous effort to become enlightened in order then to help other suffering beings achieve enlightenment and freedom.

There are many paths of Mahayana Buddhism. Tibetan Buddhists, most of them now exiled from Tibet and living in nearby India or other lands such as the United States, may use advanced meditation practices in order to develop their own inner qualities. Zen Buddhism originated in China and then grew in Japan from the thirteenth century onward. In Zen, starkly disciplined meditation practices are prescribed by a master teacher to help reveal the "natural mind," which is open and free like the sky.

Buddhism Today

At the beginning of the twenty-first century, Buddhism has captured the interest of many educated people in the West. In France, for instance, it is the most popular "new religion." Eagerness for the teachings is evident in the strength of the market for Buddhist books. A single publisher based in Boston, Massachusetts, is offering fifty titles on Tibetan Buddhism alone. Severe discipline is required to sit for hours on end, meditating on the breath or the contents of the mind, or walking while forcing the mind to concentrate only on the action of walking. This restriction on thought and activity is the antithesis of the prevailing cultural emphasis on working hard to earn money and spending it for pleasure. Often it is precisely those who have become disillusioned with the "rat race" who have turned to Buddhist practice for a sense of inner freedom and happiness.

Another aspect of contemporary Buddhism practice that is gaining ground is the restoration of women as teachers and monastics. Given

Buddhism's emphases on compassion and liberation, it is perhaps surprising that women's freedom to teach the Dharma has historically been quite limited. Although the Buddha established an order of Buddhist nuns and said that women were capable of achieving enlightenment, in the Indian culture of Buddha's time the role of women was defined entirely by their family obligations. Women were subservient to their husbands and their husbands' family. Eventually, Buddhist nuns were likewise subjected to special rules which kept them subservient to Buddhist monks. The most senior nun, for instance, must bow and defer to the newest, lowliest of monks.

It is known that during the Buddha's lifetime thousands of women forsook family life to be ordained as nuns, and many are remembered for their enlightened wisdom. As Buddhism spread eastward, many of the deities and boddhisatvas who were revered were female. Nevertheless, perhaps because of the distinctly anti-female attitude of the Theravadin monks, the order of fully ordained Buddhist nuns completely disappeared in Theravadin countries a thousand years ago. In Mahayana countries, women have been on a more equal footing in Buddhism. The influential thirteenth-century Zen master Dogen said,

> What is more worthy about a male? . . . Simply you should revere and honour the one who actualises the Dharma and do not consider the matter of being male or female.[15]

Nevertheless, in Mahayana as well, men have tended to dominate teaching of the Dharma.

As the twenty-first century dawns, the suppression of women's voice in Buddhism is lessening, especially as Buddhism has spread to countries such as the United States and Europe where women are demanding egalitarian treatment in all spheres. Keen American interest in Buddhism is accompanied by a spate of new American-born teachers, many of them women. Some are nuns who have shaved their heads and wear Buddhist robes; others live as wives and mothers in households but have been rigorously trained in meditation practices, usually by Eastern masters, and have thus been ordained to guide others. They characteristically translate the Dharma into modern terms, emphasizing their relevance for contemporary life and creating new ways of meditating.

Despite continuing opposition by some conservative Asian monks to the ordination of nuns, full ordinations of women as Buddhist monastics are being held again by masters such as Taiwan-based Master Hsing

Yun. In 1998, he presided over the full ordination of 135 nuns and fourteen monks in Bodh Gaya, where the Buddha achieved enlightenment. Master Hsing Yun emphasized to them the necessity of endurance and patience in order to survive the pressures of both power and hardships.

Hardships in the postmodern world have stimulated another feature of contemporary Buddhism: social activism based on compassion, the central Buddhist virtue. In addition to practicing meditation, many Buddhists today are marching for peace, pressing for abolition of landmines, demanding social justice, trying to stop the destruction of the natural environment, nonviolently protesting genocide. These words of the Buddha are often quoted:

> Hatred is never appeased by hatred. It is appeased by love.
> This is an eternal law. Just as a mother would protect her
> only child, even at the risk of her own life, even so let one
> cultivate a boundless heart towards all beings. Let one's
> thoughts of boundless love pervade the whole world above,
> below, and across, without any obstruction, without any
> hatred, without any enmity. Whether one stands, walks, sits,
> or lies down, as long as one is awake, one should maintain
> this mindfulness. This, they say, is to attain the blessed state
> in this very life.[16]

Close-up: *Sarvodaya*

Despite the religion's emphasis on nonviolence and compassion, Buddhists have been drawn into social conflict in parts of Asia in the wake of rapid modernization, economic collapses, and political pressures. In Sri Lanka, for instance, Buddhist monks from the majority Sinhalese community are prominent in the effort to suppress an uprising by Hindus who are trying to create a separate state for their Tamil minority. Nevertheless, in the midst of the violence, a Buddhist social program begun in the middle of the twentieth century in Sri Lanka—*Sarvodaya*—is continuing to work for rural development of Hindus and Christians as well as Buddhists.

In 1958, a Sri Lankan teacher, Dr. A. T. Ariyaratne, began developing *Sarvodaya* in his country, reinterpreting in a Buddhist way Mahatma Gandhi's ideal of a new social order which would be different from either capitalism or socialism. (Gandhi (1869–1948) helped achieve India's independence from Britain by orchestrating a campaign of nonviolent civil disobedience.) Ariyaratne defines *Sarvodaya* as "the awakening of all." He explains,

> Transcending all man-made barriers of caste, race, religion, nationality, and other ways of separating human beings, Sarvodaya serves all. Sarvodaya works to remove the causes of human physical suffering, anxiety, and fear.[17]

After organizing self-help development projects with poor villages, Ariyaratne began training Buddhist monks to help carry out the work, basing it on central Buddhist principles and the traditionally close cooperation between Buddhists monks and the villages where their communities are located. Now some 7,000 villages and 2,000 monks are involved in the work of *Sarvodaya*, carrying out projects such as building roads, irrigation canals, preschools, community kitchens, and marketing cooperatives.

Ariyaratne asserts that the cause of poverty is the feeling of individual and community powerlessness. To eliminate poverty requires individual awakening, in the context of the social, economic, and political enlightenment of the whole community. Villagers are encouraged to look carefully at their shared problems—disease, poverty, strife, stagnation, oppression—and to discover that they all stem from personal problems which keep the people from working together fruitfully. They see that it is their own egotism, distrust of each other, greed, and competitiveness which are causing their suffering. This realization then unleashes the awakening of voluntary cooperative activity to end the suffering.

Each of the Four Noble Truths and aspects of the Eightfold Path have been given immediate practical relevance to community life in *Sarvodaya*. Right mindfulness, for instance, is discussed as being always aware of the needs of the village: "Look to see what is needed—latrines, water, road...Is the food enough? Are people getting wet? Are the tools in order? Is anyone being exploited?"[18]

Dr. Ariyaratne explains the success of this work as a practical embodiment of the teachings of the Buddha:

> *Sarvodaya* signifies the awakening or liberation of one and all, without exception. "May all beings be well and happy," is the Buddhist wish. . . . In a world where greed, hatred, and ignorance are so well organized, is it possible for this thought of the well-being of all to be effectively practised for

the regeneration of the individual and society? The answer to that question lies in the lives of hundreds of thousands of village people in Sri Lanka who have embraced the *Sarvodaya* way to development.[19]

Judaism

The oldest of the major global religions which developed in the West is Judaism. Its first great patriarch, Abraham, is thought to have lived some time between 1900 and 1700 B.C.E., before the Vedas were written down in India. The spiritual traditions traced back to him now have three large branches: Judaism, Christianity, and Islam. Together, they account for over half of the world's believers. Jews themselves are not numerically significant today; only a quarter of 1 percent of the world's people are Jewish, and many people of Jewish ethnic background do not practice the religion. Nevertheless, Judaism remains important as a seminal tradition, and as the religion of the State of Israel it occupies a critical position politically.

This chart shows current followers of the world's religions. Percentages of the world's population following each religion or none, and approximate numbers of followers (in brackets), are based on statistics in The World Almanac.

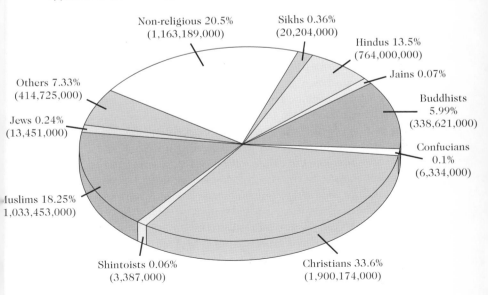

Non-religious 20.5%
(1,163,189,000)

Sikhs 0.36%
(20,204,000)

Hindus 13.5%
(764,000,000)

Jains 0.07%

Others 7.33%
(414,725,000)

Buddhists
5.99%
(338,621,000)

Jews 0.24%
(13,451,000)

Confucians
0.1%
(6,334,000)

Muslims 18.25%
1,033,453,000)

Shintoists 0.06%
(3,387,000)

Christians 33.6%
(1,900,174,000)

Traditional Beliefs and Practices

The basic tenets of Judaism are recorded in the Hebrew Bible (which Christians refer to as the "Old Testament"). The writings are regarded as sacred history, the record of God's voice. The account begins with the creation of the cosmos—actually, with two different stories of the creation—in the book of Genesis. In the first account, the earth was unformed and void until the wind or spirit of God swept over its waters. This God, who was transcendent and formless, created the material universe and then made humans in the "likeness" of the divine. They were placed as masters over all creatures of the earth.

From that time onward, according to the Hebrew Bible, history has revolved around the relationship between the Creator and the humans, and their responsibility to take care of the world. The early stories are about the patriarchs and matriarchs of a small area east of the Mediterranean Sea and their offspring. Eventually, the idea arose that these people—who were called Jews because they came from Judea—were especially chosen by God to uplift the world to the perfect harmony which God intends.

The Jewish people were repeatedly told that God had made a special **covenant** with them: "I will be your God and you shall be my people."[20] God is believed to have intervened in history in the time of Moses (approximately twelfth century B.C.E.) to free the Israelites from slavery in Egypt, to feed them as they wandered in the wilderness, to protect them in battle, and lead them successfully to a promised land of plenty. Nevertheless, neither society at large nor the Jewish people in particular became perfect, and the Jewish prophets repeatedly warned of God's wrathful displeasure with human wickedness. There were also repeated injunctions to turn away from other deities and ways of worship, and to follow the seven **Noachide laws** originally given to the legendary Adam (the first human) and Noah (the only righteous and obedient man in a time of moral decay). Forbidden were idolatry, blasphemy against God, unrestrained sexuality, murder, theft, and eating living animals. The people were also instructed to create a legal system to set clear boundaries for human behavior. In the time of Moses, God is said to have given a great number of additional commandments covering every aspect of life in detail, such as foods which can and cannot be eaten. The central commandment, however, was love of God. To this day, the injunction attributed to Moses is the major expression of Jewish faith:

Hear, O Israel, the Lord is our God, the Lord alone. You shall

love the Lord your God with all your heart and with all your
soul and with all your might.[21]

The Hebrew Bible is full of heroic figures, as well as wrongdoers.
One towering figure is King David, who rose from being a shepherd to
establishing the beginnings of a prosperous Israelite empire in around
1000 B.C.E., with Jerusalem as its capital. Many touching songs to God
which appear as the biblical book of Psalms are traditionally attributed
to David. The Psalms exemplify the special covenant of the faithful with
God:

I know, O Lord, that Your rulings are just;
  rightly have You humbled me.
May Your steadfast love comfort me
  in accordance with Your promise to Your servant.
May Your mercy reach me, that I might live,
  for Your teaching is my delight.[22]

Over time, Jerusalem fell under foreign rule and in 586 B.C.E.
Jerusalem's great Temple, focus of Jewish devotion, was destroyed by the
Babylonians. Many Jews were carried off to exile in Babylonia. A small
group who returned rebuilt the Temple, but in 70 C.E. the Second
Temple was demolished during a rebellion against Roman occupation.
The people began to gather in synagogues, or "meeting places," to read
the scriptures and worship together. Biblical scripture—the written
Torah, or "teaching"—had been declared completed; what remained
was to interpret and apply it to contemporary life. This work was undertaken—and still continues—through **rabbis**, who are teachers, decision-
makers, and creators of liturgy.

Babylon became the center of Jewish religious activity. Jews also
migrated to other countries and in time established communities
throughout Europe. There they were intellectually, spiritually, and finan-
cially active, but periodically met with terrible oppression, culminating
in the **holocaust**, the murder of nearly six million Jews by Nazi Germany
during the Second World War (1939–45). Following the holocaust, some
Jews worked to establish a Jewish state in the biblical land of Israel, as
an end to their foreign exile. However, relationships between the Israeli
settlers, the Palestinian inhabitants of the area, and neighboring countries are very tense and have often led to armed conflicts.

Despite its historical difficulties, for thousands of years Jewish spirituality has always upheld certain central principles. Judaism is strictly

monotheistic, insisting upon the oneness of God, Who created everything and is everywhere present. Along with the oneness of God, Judaism
has always preached love of God. The classic injunction, "You shall love
the Lord your God with all your heart and with all your soul and with all
your might," is to be carefully taught to one's children, and repeated
again and again in everyday life. One's life is also to be conducted according to the laws that God has given for spiritual and secular matters. And
no matter how bad things become, Jews are encouraged to believe that
some day a messiah will come to raise the Jewish people and usher in a
time of universal peace.

Judaism Today

Over the millennia, Jewish spirituality has continued to evolve in various
directions. Today Judaism is responding to modernization, globalization, and rational secularism by forms ranging from ultra-Orthodoxy to
liberal reform movements. In areas where Jews are a minority amid
mostly secular populations, many have abandoned Jewish religious practice and are Jewish only in the sense of ethnicity. Observant Jews themselves have the chance to choose from varieties of Judaism since they are
no longer constrained by tight-knit unified cultures.

Reform Judaism began in eighteenth-century Germany as an
attempt to help Jews understand their religion in modern terms rather
than rejecting it as old-fashioned. Reform congregations are popular in
the United States, where rabbis explain Judaism in universal terms and
encourage creative new ideas and ways of worship. Conservative
Judaism, which arose late in the nineteenth century in Europe and the
United States, is more oriented toward the traditional rabbinical
model, and yet it is engaged in modern critical textual analysis as part
of what it sees as a continual process of reconstructing the faith in contemporary terms. Reconstruction Judaism was developed in the United
States in the twentieth century as a rationalist movement, denying
such articles of faith as the supernatural revelation of the Torah, God's
supernatural intervention on behalf of the Jews, and the belief that
Jews are God's specially chosen people. Orthodox Jews reject all these
movements as assimilations to secular society, and instead espouse
strict adherence to authoritarian historical traditions. Orthodox
Judaism is strong in Israel, but even there, only an estimated 15 percent of Jews are strictly observant, whereas nearly 30 percent do not
observe Jewish laws at all.[23]

In contrast to traditional strictures on the role of Jewish women, twentieth-century Jewish feminists have attempted to bring women into traditionally male roles such as the position of rabbi and to illuminate women's perspectives on moral values, spirituality, and theology. They are very active, for instance, in questioning humans' relationship to the natural environment, exploring the "feminine" aspects of God, and bringing to light private traditions by which Jewish women have brought spirituality to bear on the events of their lives, such as childbirth.

Close-up: Lubavicher Hasidism

At the same time that many Jews are embracing liberal reconstructions of their faith, or no faith at all, a movement which is showing surprising strength at the turn of the twenty-first century is ultra-Orthodox Lubavicher Hasidism.

The word "Hasid" means a righteous person who is particularly close to God. The Hasidic movement appeared in Eastern Europe late in the eighteenth century, centered on charismatic leaders called *zaddiks.* First among them was the Baal Shem Tov (1700–60). His experience and emphasis was mystical attachment of the soul to God, and he stressed joyful, enthusiastic prayer and worship. Known as a healer as well as a teacher, he traveled among the Jewish communities in Eastern Europe, attracting some opposition from the religious establishment but also many followers. A Hasidic *zaddik* was revered as a guru whose power was such that he could help raise his followers to higher spiritual levels. The movement had such appeal that by the First World War (1914–18), it was the mainstay of Judaism in Europe. Before the holocaust all but destroyed the European Jewish community during the Second World War, many Hasids escaped to other countries.

The Lubavicher Hasids were among the immigrants to the United States from Lithuania. Their rabbis trace their lineage back to the Baal Shem Tov, arguing that he mystically initiated Rabbi Schneur Zalmann (1745–1812) as his successor. Schneur Zalmann was opposed both by non-Hasidic Jews and by anti-semitic non-Jews and was imprisoned by the Russian tsar. Nevertheless, he is said to have been regarded as such a great spiritual power that many high officials came for his blessings and he was soon released. His successors, all of whom carried the name Schneurson ("son of Schneur"), also spent time in Russian prisons.

After the Bolshevik Revolution of 1917, attempts were made to eliminate all religions in Russia, with a special department assigned to eliminating Jews. Synagogues were destroyed and rabbis and believers beaten, to the point that only a few rabbis were left in all of Russia. However, Lubavicher Jewry survived through underground schools which moved from town to town.

During Stalin's rule, the sixth Lubavich rabbi's communities were infiltrated by the secret police, and the rabbi was arrested and tortured. Though old and sick, he refused to abandon his spiritual practices, and prayed openly while imprisoned. He was to be executed, but he was miraculously released after three years in prison. In the mid-1970s a Jewish reawakening developed in the midst of Soviet oppression, and young Jews began again secretly to practice a traditional Jewish way of life. Although rabbis were few, Lubavicher Hasidic rabbis came from abroad disguised as tourists, and Jews met secretly in small groups to study the ancient teachings.

A very different hurdle had to be faced in America: indifference to religion. When the seventh Rabbi Schneurson carried the mission to America, he was told by other rabbis that there was no point in emphasizing traditional study of the Torah, for many Jews in the United States and Canada had abandoned their spiritual tradition and were living secular lives. One rabbi reportedly said to him, "Hair will sooner grow on the palm of my hand than Jews will start to study Torah." Much to the contrary, Lubavich emphasis on the Torah has proved to have strong appeal, and has encouraged many nonobservant Jews to return to their Jewish spiritual roots.

According to Hasidism, if things are awry in the world, it is because Jews have not lived up to their responsibility for uplifting humanity to perfection. The best response to corruption in society is therefore for individual Jews to practice the traditional commandments and to cling more closely to God. The charismatic seventh Lubavich Rabbi Schneurson developed an assertive outreach program. He sent crusade vans equipped with modern telecommunications equipment to universities and other places where religiously estranged Jews might be found. He also kept in touch personally with his followers through a battery of telephones.

Initially rejected as odd extremists, Hasidim with their traditional dress and strict practices have earned a reputation as "super Jews," as models for Jewish life. Finding materialism and secularism unsatisfying and meaningless, an increasing number of Jews have been attracted to the clearly defined values and traditional living patterns of Lubavicher Hasidism. Some women find that the traditional patriarchal definitions of the roles of men and women provide a refuge from the confusions of modern sexual freedom and broken families. A strong sense of community has been carefully nurtured, centered on the rabbi. When the seventh Lubavich rabbi died in 1994 without naming a successor, his followers were deeply shocked. Some now visit his grave site as a place for pilgrimage, seeking miraculous aid and consolation. They believe that he will rise from the dead as the long-awaited messiah and at last deliver the Jewish people from exile. At the turn of the century, this ultra-Orthodox version of Judaism continues alongside contrasting liberal interpretations of the faith.

Christianity

Perhaps more than any other religion, Christianity is centered on the life, teachings, and even death of its founder, Jesus (c. 4 B.C.E.–30 C.E.). He was the son of a humble carpenter of whom little is known, although his mother Mary is highly venerated. He was a Jew, and he referred often to the Torah. Some Jews recognized him as their long-awaited messiah, but many did not. He traveled only within a limited area of Judea and Galilee no more than 100 miles long spreading his message. He taught for perhaps only three years, and then was crucified. Nothing appears about him in historical records of the times. Nonetheless, the new movement which developed in his name—Christianity—now has the most followers of any religion in the world. As the twenty-first century begins, over one-third of all human beings—nearly two billion people—call themselves Christians.

Traditional Beliefs and Practices

Part of the appeal of Jesus lies in the power of his teachings. They were probably carried orally and then written down perhaps forty to fifty years after his death as four gospels (books of "good news") forming the heart of the Christian Bible. This scripture is also made up of the Hebrew Bible (which Christians call the "Old Testament"), plus accounts and letters of the early Christian leaders' missions after Jesus died and then reportedly miraculously reappeared to his followers.

The gospels attribute many miracles to Jesus—healings of incurable conditions, walking on water, feeding thousands with only a few loaves and fishes, bringing the dead back to life, turning water into wine. These were said to be signs of the coming of the kingdom of God, and could also be interpreted metaphorically. Miraculous offerings of bread and wine prefigured the "Last Supper," when before his death, Jesus instituted a ceremony for his remembrance based on sharing of wine and bread as if they were his very blood and his body. Christians believe that these were sacrificially given in love so that his followers might be inwardly transformed and saved.

Jesus based his teachings on the Torah, but extended the earlier commandments into truly radical ethics. Once when a large number of people had come to listen to him and to be healed, he delivered a major discourse, known as the "Sermon on the Mount" (Matthew 5–7). According to the gospel account, he said,

> Love your enemies; do good to those who hate you; bless those who curse you; pray for those who treat you spitefully. When a man hits you on the cheek, offer him the other cheek too; when a man takes your coat, let him have your shirt as well. Give to everyone who asks you; when a man takes what is yours, do not demand it back. Treat others as you would like them to treat you. If you love only those who love you, what credit is that to you? Even sinners love those who love them. . . . [24]

Jesus's main commandment was to love God and our fellow humans sincerely, rather than professing piety without practicing it. He taught that God is merciful and forgiving to those who truly repent of their sins; those who make an outward show of piety and consider themselves superior cannot draw close to God. Those who are especially blessed are the gentle in spirit, the sorrowful, the pure in heart, those who know they need God, who long to do what is right, who are merciful to others, who make peace, who suffer persecution for the cause of right. Our prayers should be utterly private and based in the faith that "our Father" knows what we need without our asking. We should do good deeds so secretly that when we give to the needy, one hand does not even know what the other is doing. We should seek the narrow gate to the kingdom of God: "The gate that leads to life is small and the road is narrow, and those who find it are few."[25]

What is this kingdom of God, or kingdom of Heaven, to which Jesus so often referred? Jesus lived at a time of fervent expectations among Jews that a messiah would come to rescue them from the bad times under Roman oppression and establish the rule of the God of Israel.

Jesus repeatedly spoke of the imminent fulfillment of these expectations. His miraculous healings and casting out of evil spirits were taken as indications that God's full power was breaking through into the world. But the kingdom of which Jesus spoke was not a political entity. Jesus often referred to it mystically, through **parables**, teaching stories based on familiar examples. Sometimes he referred to it as an **apocalypse**, an end-time of terrible distress in the world, following which:

> At the end of time the Son of Man will send out his angels, who will gather out of his kingdom whatever makes men stumble, and all whose deeds are evil, and these will be thrown into the blazing furnace, the place of wailing and grinding of teeth. And then the righteous will shine as brightly as the sun in the kingdom of their Father.[26]

And sometimes Jesus seemed to refer to the kingdom of God as an inner state of bliss which can be obtained only by turning solely toward God. He explained,

> The kingdom of Heaven is like treasure lying buried in a field. The man who found it, buried it again; and for sheer joy went and sold everything he had, and bought that field.[27]

Although Jesus preached love and forgiveness, the gospels are full of vitriolic statements about the Jewish rabbis, priests, and legalists. It is possible that some of this material was added later to the Christian Bible to differentiate between the new Christians and Jews who were not followers of Jesus. Nevertheless, the attacks on religious managers ring with universal prophetic truth. According to the gospel accounts, Jesus reportedly said that humble children, repentant tax-gatherers, and prostitutes would enter the kingdom of God before the hypocritical religious authorities. He confronted them with the spiritual truth of their own scriptures, and referred to them as "blind guides, and if one blind man guides another they will both fall into the ditch."[28]

The priests and the Roman authorities seem to have collaborated in sentencing Jesus to death by crucifixion, on religious charges of blasphemy, for calling himself the Son of God, and civil charges of sedition, claiming that he called himself "King of the Jews." He was beaten, crowned with thorns, paraded through the streets, and nailed to a cross to die. He had reportedly foreseen his death and had referred to it as a sacrifice by which all who believed in him could be redeemed.

After Jesus was crucified, he was said to have miraculously resurrected from death, revealing his divinity. When he reappeared to his disheartened disciples, they became convinced that he had been no ordinary human being, and that he had the power to lift others as well into eternal life, into the "kingdom" of goodness, love, and peace, in this life as well as the life after death. When Jesus reappeared, he blessed his disciples to carry on his mission with divine authority and spiritual power. They were further empowered by an event called the **Pentecost**, a miraculous experience of the spirit of God falling upon them, like tongues of fire. Whereas Jesus had preached primarily to Jews, the resurrected Jesus is said to have told the disciples,

> Full authority in heaven and on earth has been committed to me. Go forth therefore and make all nations my disciples; baptize men everywhere in the name of the Father and Son and the Holy Spirit, and teach them to observe all that I have commanded you. And be assured, I am with you always, to the end of time.[29]

As Jesus had warned, the disciples met with stiff opposition and persecution. Yet one of their persecutors, Paul, had a vision of Jesus which so transformed him that he became the most influential figure in the spread of Christianity. From approximately 50 to 60 C.E., Paul traveled extensively throughout the Mediterranean world, preaching his interpretation of the gospel. He tried to convince Jews that Jesus was the Messiah (Hebrew) or **Christ** (Greek), the savior for whom they had been waiting, an incarnation of God who had come for the salvation of all humanity, not only for Jews. He tried to convince people of other religions, such as worshipers of the old gods, that they could be saved by inward repentance of their sins and faith in the grace of Jesus, rather than by outward conformity to religious laws.

Paul's interpretations of the nature and role of Jesus became very influential in shaping the theology of Christianity. After several hundred years of severe persecution, it became the state religion of the huge Roman Empire. From there, it was spread throughout the world in accordance with the missionary goal attributed to Jesus.

Christianity is not monolithic, however. Over time, many versions of Christianity have developed. Although all are based on faith in God through the intercession of Jesus, there are now around 21,000 independent Church denominations. Historically, most have evolved from three major branches of the global Christian Church. In 1054, there was a formal split between the Roman Church and the Eastern Orthodox Church. Then again in the sixteenth century, Protestants began to split away from the Roman Catholic Church. Despite attempts to reunite Christians, there remain many areas of theological and organizational disagreements among them.

Because Christianity is based on faith in Jesus as savior, as intercessor between the believer and God, Christian groups have created various methods of professing and reinforcing this faith. From the early centuries of Christianity, systematic statements of faith, or **creeds**, have been carefully developed by church councils. There is also the ceremony of **baptism,** ritual cleansing with or immersion in water to remove one's sins. After being thus cleansed, according to a recent pronouncement by the World Council of Churches, Christians "are raised here and now to a new life in the power of the resurrection of Jesus Christ."[30]

A third major ritual assertion of faith in Jesus is Holy Communion or **Eucharist**. It is one of the major **sacraments** in all forms of Christianity. The word "sacrament" means "mystery." The sacraments are holy rites which are considered capable of transmitting the mystery of Jesus to those who would worship him. In Holy Communion, the unseen Christ is said to become present in the bread and wine which are consumed in remembrance of his body and blood, sacrificially given as a "covenant" so that many might be forgiven of their sins. In many churches, this ceremony is reserved only for those who have been baptized as Christians in that particular version of the faith.

Christianity Today

With its 21,000 different denominations, Christianity is the subject of many contemporary variations on the mission begun by Jesus. As Christianity has spread, it has become **multicultural** and today individual cultures are increasingly developing their own special expressions of the faith. For instance, in contrast to more staid European models of worship, twentieth-century African Christian churches introduced drumming and dancing into their services. After centuries of being embarrassed about their subjugation by European colonizers, African Christian theologians have begun to value African inspiration in interpreting Christian faith. Since the 1960s, theologians in Africa and Latin America have been developing **liberation theology,** emphasizing social action to help liberate the poor from social and political injustices. Feminist theology is likewise being developed by intellectuals who are challenging the patriarchal models which have long characterized Christian thinking and organizations; they are asserting the relevance of women's religious experiences and perspectives. A men's movement is also gaining strength, with such manifestations as the Promise Keepers, in which largely white, middle-class Protestant men gather for large stadium rallies to confront and resolve their postmodern feelings of powerlessness and isolation, and their failures to keep their promises to their families and their Churches. Finally, the ecumenical movement which began in the middle of the twentieth century is still actively trying to build bridges of fellowship between Churches of different Christian denominations, as well as with people of other faiths.

At the same time as such liberalizing movements are opening doors, conservative Christian movements are trying to close them. Christian Fundamentalism arose early in the twentieth century in the United States and is still a powerful force (see p. 21). Fundamentalists protest against the modern scientific approach to the Bible and to matters of faith, such as the creation of the world by God. They assert what they considered the "fundamentals" of Christian faith, including literal belief in the Bible as inspired and authoritative, belief in Jesus's divinity and his miracles, belief in Jesus's physical resurrection, belief in Jesus's sacrificial atonement for the sins of those who place their faith in him, and belief that Jesus will soon come again into the world. In the last twenty years of the twentieth century, Christian Fundamentalism has joined with conservative political forces to become the Religious Right, playing a major role in American politics and actively opposing liberal tendencies, such as the ecumenical movement and the pro-choice movement with reference to abortion.

Cutting across these polarities and across denominational lines are two other vibrant trends in contemporary Christianity: evangelism and charismatic experience. Ever since the early days of the Christian church, many Christians have felt that they should spread the message of the gospel and convert people to Christianity. This evangelical mission gained momentum again in the twentieth century, especially in Protestant denominations. They may be tolerant toward other religions but ultimately they feel that only through faith in Jesus can humanity be saved. Evangelicals carry out their "urgent task" through missionaries, businesspeople who testify about Jesus as they travel, Christian radio and television stations, audiotapes, videotapes, movies, and literature in the local languages.

The charismatic movement in its present form developed in the 1960s, though its roots are older. Its followers seek the dynamic personal experience of the Holy Spirit, and during worship look to engage their emotions and heart rather than their intellect. Signs of the presence of the Holy Spirit are said to include the ability to heal, to prophesy, and perhaps to speak in tongues. Charismatic renewal has appeared within traditional congregations and also in new independent movements, with strong participation by the laity, who offer more visceral styles of prayer and worship.

Close-up: Pentecostalism

An antecedent and continuing manifestation of the charismatic renewal movement is Pentecostalism. The term refers to the Pentecost experienced by Jesus's disciples after his death. According to the biblical account,

> Suddenly a sound like the blowing of a violent wind came
> from heaven and filled the whole house where they were
> sitting. They saw what seemed to be tongues of fire that
> separated and came to rest on each of them. All of them
> were filled with the Holy Spirit and began to speak in other
> tongues as the Spirit enabled them.[31]

Thus the early disciples were empowered to teach the gospel and convert people to faith in Jesus. They miraculously began to speak in the various languages of the people in the crowd that gathered.

The letters of Paul to new Christian congregations indicate that the apostle Paul also had this "gift of the Spirit" and that it was common among the congregations he developed, but that listeners could not understand the "language" being spoken. Paul explained that they were not speaking to humans, but to God. The phenomenon of speaking in tongues was understood as evidence that a person had been "baptized" by the Holy Spirit, especially if his or her life was also transformed. Today's Pentecostalists feel they are experiencing a second Pentecost, like the first apostles of Jesus. They also feel that their movement fulfills the prophecy of the Hebrew prophet Joel about the "end times." The prophet claimed that God said to him,

> The day shall come when I will pour out my spirit on all
> mankind; your sons and your daughters shall prophesy, your
> old men shall dream dreams, and your young men see visions.[32]

The Pentecostal movement originated in the United States near the beginning of the twentieth century from several different roots. One is the 1880 miracle healing of Charles Mason, the son of former slaves. As he lay dying from tuberculosis, he reportedly experienced the radiant presence of God and was cured. From that point until his death in 1961, he was revered as a mystic, an evangelist, a model of piety, and the leader of the Church of God in Christ, which he founded in 1897.

In 1906, Mason had attended the **Azusa Street Revival** meeting in Los Angeles, another of the roots of today's Pentecostalism. Despite racial segregation in the society at large, the Azusa Street Revival united believers from all races, under the inspiration of William J. Seymour, a self-taught African-American minister with only one good eye. Those who came to his revival meetings were primarily working-class people facing poverty and unemployment as Los Angeles rapidly changed from a Mexican-American farming town to a large industrial city. The spiritual power they felt washing over them at Azusa Street gave them an inner sense of assurance. Charles Mason described his experience at the revival meeting:

> There came a wave of glory into me, and all of my being was filled with the glory of the Lord. So when I had gotten myself straight on my feet there came a light which enveloped my entire being above the brightness of the sun. . . . My language changed and no word could I speak in my own tongue. Oh, I was filled with the glory of my Lord. My soul was then satisfied. I rejoiced in Jesus my Savior, whom I love so dearly.[33]

Pentecostalist churches attempt to arouse in people the same fervent faith, piety, and power ascribed to the early Christians and expected in the "end times." Charles Mason facilitated these Pentecostal expectations by combining evangelical themes with African patterns of worshiping. Churches that he and his missionaries initiated rang with exuberant singing, praising, and testifying by members of the congregation, with drumming and preaching that called forth spontaneous responses from the people. He also encouraged them to believe in their ability to accomplish things with God's help. The urban storefront churches gave way to very large structures built by black craftsmen, paid for by contributions from the mostly black congregations.

Leaders of some white Pentecostal churches attacked Mason for introducing "voodoo culture" into Christianity. He was also jailed for preaching pacifism during World War I. Nevertheless, his movement continued to grow, and now every major city in the United States has large Churches of God in Christ with over a thousand members each. The largest, in Los Angeles, has 13,000 members, 155 paid staff members, and a yearly budget of $8 million. The pastor explains that they try to make the church "user-friendly" by providing plenty of parking space, good music, and sincere preaching. The commitment to urban ministry remains strong. On Friday nights, church members in San Diego fan out seeking converts in the red-light district, encouraging prostitutes and drug addicts to turn to God. Some 60 percent of the members of the San Diego church were once street people.

The primarily black Church of God in Christ is so successful that it can no longer be scorned by white Pentecostalists. In 1994, the "Memphis Miracle" occurred: Leaders of white Pentecostalist denominations went to Memphis to ask forgiveness for having excluded the Church of God in Christ from their fellowship. They dissolved their organization and formed the new multiracial Pentecostal Charismatic Churches of North America. Church of God in Christ Bishop Ithiel Clemmons was placed in charge of the super-group.

Newly integrated, black and white Pentecostalists are trying to set aside racist attitudes in order to worship and work together. One method being tried is to send teams of black and white Pentecostalists into prisons to offer worship services and also to try to help the prisoners deal with their anger and to rehabilitate them. Bishop Clemmons sums up the success of the movement thus:

> The Church of God in Christ is possibly the prime example of
> the self-help tradition in America. It is a people that started
> as the children of slaves—share-croppers, farmers, oppressed
> people. They asked no one for anything. They migrated to
> the major cities of America and became successful. They felt
> that the experience of the baptism of the Holy Ghost took
> the apostrophe and the t from the word "can't," so they
> could say, "We can do all things through Christ who
> strengthens us."[34]

Since 1982, the Church of God in Christ has been adding an average of 600 new congregations each year, with a current total of 6.75 million members. There are now an estimated 450 million Pentecostalists worldwide. In the former Soviet Union, Pentecostalism has maintained a strong presence since the 1920s, even during the years of severe religious oppression. Pentecostal missionary activities are also vibrant in South America. In the United States, Pentecostalism is the fastest-growing of all Christian denominations, and particularly so in urban areas.

Islam

Whereas Christians regard Jesus as the divine son of God, Muslims refuse to ascribe divinity to their founder, the Prophet Muhammad (c. 570 C.E.–632 C.E.). The focus in Islam is on love for and fear of **Allah** (God), whose attributes are many but who is only One.

Muhammad was an orphan from a poor clan, raised as a shepherd in what is now the Kingdom of Saudi Arabia. When he was twenty-five, he married his employer, Khadijah, who became his strongest supporter. It was reportedly his habit to withdraw to a cave for spiritual contemplation. On one such retreat when he was forty years old, the angel Gabriel is said to have appeared to the illiterate Muhammad and insisted that he begin reciting as the angel dictated. Over a period of twenty-three years, Muhammad continued to receive these revelations, in sometimes intensely painful spiritual experiences. They formed a sacred corpus which was written down during the Prophet's lifetime as the **Qur'an** ("reciting").

Muhammad is seen as a beautiful example to follow and is highly venerated in popular piety, but he denied having any divine powers. Nor do Muslims regard Muhammad as the only Prophet. He is seen as the last of a continuing tradition of prophets beginning with Adam and including Moses and Jesus. Abraham is recognized as the patriarch of Islam as well as of Judaism and Christianity. According to the Qur'an, Abraham and his son Ishmael constructed a sacred building, the Ka'ba, in what is now Mecca. It became a pilgrimage site for Arabic tribes, but over time they turned away from Abrahamic monotheism and installed idols of many local divinities in the Ka'ba.

When Muhammad announced revelations criticizing the worship of many deities, he was scorned and stoned by the religious authorities who were running the Ka'ba and making money from the pilgrims. Few people believed him. During this time of persecution, he reportedly experienced the Night of Ascension, in which he rose through the seven heavens, meeting previous prophets and teachers from Adam to Jesus, and was blessed with the divine presence. Afterward, people who recognized him as a prophet called him to what is now called Medina ("City of the

Prophet"), which became his spiritual and political center. There his following increased, until eight years later, he returned triumphantly to Mecca, removed the idols from the Ka'ba, and established it again as a center for monotheistic worship. According to the Qur'an, monotheism—belief in one God—is the original and basic religion of humanity.

Traditional Beliefs and Practices

The essence of the Qur'an is affirmation of the reality and oneness of Allah, "Most Gracious, Most Merciful," and the dire fate of those who do not heed the message of Allah, as conveyed by the Prophet. The most essential virtue espoused by the Qur'an is submission to the will of Allah. Thus the name Islam, which means "surrender." And what is the will of Allah? According to the Qur'an, God has sent many messengers with the same eternal message:

> They are ordered naught else than to serve Allah,
> Keeping religion pure for Him
> As naturally upright and true people,
> To establish worship,
> And to give in charity to the needy.
> This is the true religion.[35]

According to the Qur'anic revelations, those people who do not repent and turn away from evil will be confronted with their misdeeds and grievously punished in the life hereafter. For the righteous who have heeded the message of the prophets, paradise awaits.

Not only is there only one God; there is only one human family. Islam recognizes no racial distinctions. Jews and Christians have also been recipients of God's message through their prophets, as recorded in their revealed scriptures, although according to the Qur'an, their followers have introduced some mistaken doctrines. One example is the Christian worship of Jesus:

> It is not possible
> That a man, to whom
> Is given the Book and Wisdom
> And the Prophetic Office
> Should say to people,
> "Be ye my worshippers

Rather than Allah's."
On the contrary, (he would say),
"Be ye worshippers of Him."[36]

Nonetheless, the Qur'an is full of praise for figures such as Jesus, his mother Mary, Moses, Noah, and Abraham and insists that no one should be forced to change his or her religion.

The practice of Islam is outwardly shaped by conformity to five spiritual "pillars," plus observance of prescribed social laws. The first pillar is profession of the oneness of God and the messengership of Muhammad. Although Islam was not to be spread coercively, the faithful were obliged to share the *da'wa*, the call to Islam. Muslims are encouraged not only to love and revere Allah but also to tell others about the power and mercy of Allah, in order to help them find the straight path.

The second pillar is a program of five daily prayers. They are intended to strengthen one's belief in Allah, and to awaken goodness and extinguish evil inwardly. The prayers are best recited along with other believers in a mosque, with the faithful lined up facing Mecca. They stand and bow shoulder to shoulder without social distinctions, but with men and women usually separate. Again and again, the people prostrate themselves before Allah.

The third pillar is fasting, especially during the lunar month of Ramadan, when the Qur'anic revelations to the Prophet began. Each year, the faithful abstain from food, drink, sex, and violent actions from dawn to sunset for the entire month, to achieve inner purification and mastery of desires and emotions.

The fourth pillar is giving in charity at least 2½ percent of one's income after basic expenses, to help balance differences in income within society and to "purify" one's earnings.

The fifth pillar is **hajj**, pilgrimage to the holy city of Mecca. All Muslims are expected to try to make the pilgrimage at least once in their lifetime. For this purpose, approximately two million pilgrims now arrive together in Mecca each year at the appointed time, so special structures have been built to accommodate the huge crowds. Hajj involves many ritual actions in remembrance of Allah and Muslim history, including circling the Ka'ba en masse. Muslims from around the world meet each other as one family, dressed alike in simple unsewn cloth, and thence return to their communities with renewed inspiration and an awareness of the global scope of their brother- and sisterhood.

The traditional pilgrimage to Mecca is now typically undertaken by jet. On board a Saudi aircraft, two pilgrims break their Ramadan fast with airplane dinners.

Islam Today

Islam had great appeal during the lifetime of the Prophet, and it spread rapidly, giving rise to many advanced cultures. By 1500 C.E. it had spread beyond the Arabic region in which it originated, to Africa, Spain, Central Asia, India, Malaysia, and Indonesia. Nevertheless, Western colonial expansionism eventually swept many of these areas. Indonesia, for instance, became the Dutch East Indies, Britain ruled India, and North Africa was controlled by the French. During the nineteenth century, Muslim thinkers reflected painfully upon the weakness of their community in the face of Western political and economic domination.

As the colonial empires broke up during the twentieth century, a variety of independent Muslim nation-states emerged. To a certain extent, they reflect an early division among the Prophet's followers between Sunnis (who regard themselves as bearers of the orthodox tradition) and the less numerous Shi'ites (who recognize a different lineage of successors). But contemporary scholars are de-emphasizing this split and looking more carefully at the unique characteristics of each Muslim nation-state. Turkey, for instance, has embraced a degree of secular separation between religion and the state. Theologically conservative Saudi Arabia has become a wealthy oil state which uses much of its revenues to improve the living standards of its people and to develop huge modern facilities for the millions of pilgrims to Mecca and Medina. Pakistan is relatively poor but is home to many leading intellectuals. Iran had become modernized, but under an oppressive ruler; his overthrow in 1979 brought forth a version of Islam as a continuing revolutionary movement challenging the secular effects of modernization. Indonesia, home to more Muslims than any other country, established its government on principles of religious pluralism rather than tying it to Islam. After the breakdown of Indonesia's prosperous but corrupt economy, Muslim leadership might assert itself.

Transcending such national variations, late in the twentieth century a spirit of Muslim resurgence has emerged globally. Attendance at mosques is increasing, and in Turkey alone around 1,000 new mosques are now being built yearly. There is a widespread desire to determine the relevance of Islam in today's circumstances, and to develop a new social order based on Muslim ideals. In Muslim societies, behaviors are becoming more traditional again, with a return to more modest clothing, more faithful observance of the pillars of Islam, and the development of Islamic models of education which are overtly spiritual rather than secular. In Taliban-controlled Afghanistan, the effort to establish a pure Muslim state has included such innovations as a ban on clapping in a soccer stadium. Instead, onlookers are to cheer equally for both sides by shouting, "Allah Ho Akbar!"—"God is the Greatest!"

This Muslim resurgence includes efforts to apply **shariah**—Muslim law as it has evolved in various cultural contexts—instead of secular codes of law. *Shariah* is a matter of interpretation, however, rather than a singular set of laws. The veiling of women, for instance, is not a clearcut injunction. In fact, in the context of a highly patriarchal tribal culture, the Prophet Muhammad and the Qur'an made groundbreaking efforts to protect women and establish their rights. In a society where they had been treated as possessions, women were given the right to inherit and own property, for instance. But over time, certain Qur'anic suggestions regarding women have been interpreted as justifying their seclusion and veiling. According to the Qur'an, women should lower their gaze and modestly cover their bodies when in public—perhaps to protect them from men's unwanted attention. However, in extremist Muslim societies, women have been ordered to cover themselves from head to toe in heavy garments and face veil when they travel in public, or even to stay totally sequestered at home. Muslim women in more liberal cultures move about freely and do not adopt such heavy veiling, but typically wear modest clothing with a scarf or veil covering their hair and neck.

What happens in the Muslim world is of great significance globally, for Islam is now the second most widely practiced religion in the world (second only to Christianity). It is also the fastest-growing of the global religions.

Close-up: "Black Muslims" Become Muslims

In this context, it is interesting to look at the development of Islam within the United States. Islam reached North America by the eighteenth century or perhaps earlier. Initially it arrived through immigration and the importing of slaves from Africa. It is now thought that some 14 to 20 percent of the slaves were Muslims. Some were apparently literate in Arabic; some refused to eat pork or drink alcohol, in line with Muslim tradition. However, the slaves were not free to practice their ancestral faiths openly; forced to convert to Christianity, they retained few traces of their religious heritages. In the late nineteenth century, waves of immigration brought significant numbers of Muslims to North America from the Middle East, but not until the twentieth century did African-Americans begin paying attention to the possibility that their ancestors might have been Muslims.

The first to call African-Americans' attention to Islam was a poor man from North Carolina, who changed his name from Timothy Drew to Noble Drew Ali. In 1913, he established the Moorish-American Science Temple in Newark, New Jersey, to help oppressed African-Americans develop a sense of identity and pride. He taught them that Christianity is the religion of white Europeans and their descendants, whereas they should regard themselves as being Moors, Muslims from North Africa. His movement was eventually succeeded by other similar groups.

A major new initiative was begun soon after Noble Drew Ali died in 1929, by W. F. Muhammad. He may have come from Turkey or Iran, but said he was born in Mecca. His teachings were not close to mainstream Islam, but he insisted that African-Americans had been detached from their real identity as Muslims and should return to it. He called his movement "The Lost-Found Nation of Islam in the Wilderness of North America." The wilderness was a metaphor for being lost in a secular materialistic culture which neither observed Islamic principles, nor honored dark-skinned people. Leadership of this lost and found black Nation of Islam was given to Elijah Muhammad from Georgia, whom W. F. Muhammad labeled the "Messenger of God." In contrast to the oneness of all humans and all prophets asserted by the Qur'an, Elijah Muhammad preached hatred of white people as agents of Satan. His mission had strong appeal to those who had long been suffering and poverty-stricken under white domination. Mosques and temples were built in depressed urban areas, and the call to conversion and transformation was carried into the prison system. It reached the highest professionals and intellectuals in the African-African community as well. Elijah Muhammad insisted that people totally detach themselves from the degradations of the past and commit themselves fully to a life of hard work, high morality, and traditional gender roles. Thus they would rise in self-esteem and also in economic independence.

"Black Muslims" became respected within the black community for their high standards of character, and they were instrumental in decreasing drug abuse in the inner cities. But Elijah Muhammad's mission met with criticism not only from white Christians but also from immigrant Muslims. They regarded it as racist, and therefore not in keeping with the original Muslim doctrine of the oneness of all peoples. Elijah Muhammad's chief disciple, Malcolm X, discovered from his pilgrimage to Mecca that this was so: His teacher's explanation of Islam was different from mainstream Islam. In Mecca Malcolm X experienced the brotherhood of believers, without racial distinctions. He thus discarded the idea that the white race was fundamentally evil. Then he learned that his teacher had been having extramarital sexual liaisons, contrary to his insistence on chastity. Disillusioned, Malcolm X severed his relationship with the Nation of Islam, and then was assassinated in 1965 during a religious rally. Nevertheless, his legacy remains. Not only has he become a cult hero, but also his desire to return "black Muslims" to the Muslim fold has come to pass.

The successor to Elijah Muhammad is his son, Warith Deen Muhammad, who had been influenced by Malcolm X. When Warith Deen Muhammad assumed leadership, he began trying to eliminate the gap between the Nation of Islam and traditional Islam. In place of racist doctrines, he instituted teaching of the Qur'an. Slowly, the Nation of Islam gained respect from orthodox Muslims, and in 1985, it was officially integrated into the general community of Muslims in the United States. No longer are followers "black Muslims." They are simply Muslims.

At the same time, Elijah Muhammad's racially oriented version of Islam has been maintained as a separate **sect** carrying the name of the

Nation of Islam, under the leadership of Louis Farrakhan, a charismatic speaker who urges Muslims to unite in resisting modern secular ills. His attacks on white oppression keep his movement on the fringe of Islam.

No matter which version of Islam they are following, the situation of American women who convert to the faith is somewhat problematic. They are usually lectured first of all about covering themselves. They discover that many mosques and Muslim centers do not welcome women for worship, nor are education and ambition encouraged in women. What they do learn about Islam comes from men who may not be fully knowledgeable about its tenets and nuances. For African-American women who turned to Islam at least partly to develop self-pride, the commandments to become invisible are difficult adjustments. At the same time, they find that non-Muslims stare at and harass them at work because they cover their hair. Some are told that such dress does not fit the "company image," and thus they lose their jobs. Nevertheless, many women converts to Islam are glad to adopt a sheltered role as homemaker, trying to create a stable family life in which children are protected from the perceived evils of the surrounding culture and raised in reverence for Allah.

By now, four generations have passed since the first African-Americans converted to Islam. What began for some as a negative response to racism in the culture is by now a many-faceted minority religion, in which believers strive to maintain stricter moral standards than those of the mainstream society. Islam is still little-understood in North America by non-Muslims, and Muslims of all backgrounds face difficulties in obeying the commandment to pray five times daily and to fast during the month of Ramadan. Their holy days are not treated as legitimate holidays, but they are forced to take time off work and schooling for the observance of Christian holidays. Many social observers are thus calling for increased sensitivity among American non-Muslims to the growing minority in their midst, for there are predictions that by 2015, Islam will be the second largest religion in the United States.

Conclusion

This survey of five of the world's major religions, along with indigenous spiritual traditions, reveals that many people are turning to religion for strength and guidance in the midst of a rapidly changing world. To their followers, the teachings given so long ago are not archaic; they are relevant and useful today despite—and perhaps even because of—the contemporary pressures of modernization and globalization. Some of the most vibrant expressions of religions today are those movements which fill particular contemporary needs.

From our close-up examples, we can see that Neo-paganism—a somewhat freely invented version of the reassertion of indigenous spirituality—offers an antidote to feelings of alienation from nature and from spiritual roots. Both Hindu "fundamentalism" and more liberal meditation-based movements such as the Self-Realization Fellowship are attempts to reapply some of the ancient teachings of Sanatana Dharma and find strength therein today. Buddha's classic teachings are now of great interest among intellectuals around the world as therapy for post-modern malaise and as a basis for efforts at social reform, such as *Sarvodaya*. Resurgence of interest in Judaism ranges from liberal feminism to ultra-conservative Lubavicher Hasidism. Vibrant Christian movements run the gamut from rigid and exclusive fundamentalism to emotional Pentecostalism, which is crossing racial barriers in love for Jesus and giving special uplift to those who are economically excluded by modernization. Islam is undergoing worldwide resurgence, with special appeal in the United States to the African-American community as support for a life of traditional values.

Having taking general and close-up looks at manifestations of global religions today, we now turn in the next chapter to examining how new religious movements are arising amidst older forms, how they are spreading and maintaining themselves. We are living in fluid and dynamic times in which these processes are very common.

New Religious Movements | 3

During the nineteenth and twentieth centuries, many new religions appeared, increasing the complexity of the religious make-up of the planet. Thousands have sprung up since the middle of the twentieth century alone, since times of social change are fertile ground for new movements. The modern spirit of individualism, fostered particularly in the industrialized economies, has further opened the field for people to embrace any religion that appeals to them—old or new, from anywhere in the world—rather than automatically following their parents' religion. In industrialized, urban Japan, an estimated 30 percent of the population have adopted new religious movements rather than the long-established religions of Shintoism and Buddhism.

New religious movements are extremely diverse, so generalizations that will encompass them all are few. However, in this chapter we will look at the processes by which new religions arise and might eventually become organized into continuing movements. As in Chapter 2, we will first analyze the processes in general and then take a close-up look at examples of new religions which have lasted long enough for us to discern some patterns in their formation and perpetuation, and whose vibrancy may yet carry them into the future.

For the purposes of this discussion, we will define new religious movements as those which arose within the past two centuries and are continuing today, and which are not overtly part of the mainstream in long-established religions. This does not mean that they arose independently of earlier faiths. In nearly every new religious movement can be found traces of the past. Professor Timothy Miller, a specialist in new religious movements, asserts, "Human culture is always evolving and reinventing its own past and present. There is no cultural vacuum from which anything truly new under the sun could arise."[1] Nor are the processes by which religions arise new. Those religions which are today's major global religions were once new, and once faced similar hurdles as are facing today's new religious movements.

Founders of New Religions

With many strong religions already existing and deeply entrenched in societies, how do new voices arise proclaiming new truths? And who listens to them? Today there is a great spate of people claiming to be hearing the voice of God or prophesying a grim future for the planet. Out of this chorus—be it holy or unholy—which voices command the attention of others? How do other people decide whether new would-be prophets are genuine or self-deluded?

When Muhammad began to share revelations which he said had been given to him from Allah by an angel, few believed him at first. His claim that eventually the dead would be resurrected to face a terrible Day of Judgement was particularly unappealing. The entrenched religious authorities ridiculed and stoned him. Only his wife, his cousin, one friend, and a slave were convinced that he was speaking divine truth. Perhaps one of the most convincing features of his early mission was that, though illiterate, he was reciting powerful and beautiful verses which carried their own power of persuasion. He also had a prior reputation for honesty and integrity. Thus it was that a group of pilgrims asked him to join them and help them solve the communal tensions in their city. He drew up a constitution and then led the people successfully in battle against the attacking Meccans. According to tradition, the Prophet threw a handful of pebbles at them, and since his hand was empowered by Allah, the Meccans were defeated. From these indications, we can distinguish several reasons why people began to follow the Prophet Muhammad: He said he was receiving divine revelations, which to some held the power of truth, he was a respected figure, he was politically astute, and miracles seemed to occur around him.

Another convincing quality in many founders of major religious movements is their willingness to sacrifice their own comfort for the sake of helping humanity. Buddha and Moses gave up kingdoms to help those who were suffering. The Ninth Sikh Guru and Jesus gave their lives.

The special qualities which draw people to a new religious founder are in each case unique. For instance, Muhammad's political acumen is not typical of the founders of all religious movements. But two leadership qualities which are perceived in many leaders of new movements are charisma and alleged reception of divine revelations.

Charismatic Leadership

Charisma is defined as great charm, an aura of magnetism, the ability to inspire followers with enthusiasm and devotion. More formally, the early twentieth-century scholar Max Weber, whose analyses are fundamentals of the sociology of religion, used the word "charisma" to refer to "a certain quality of an individual personality by virtue of which he is set apart from ordinary men and treated as endowed with supernatural, superhuman, or at least specifically exceptional powers or qualities."[2]

Charisma is a rare quality which automatically creates leadership and attracts followers. A living Indian guru, Amrityananda Ma, does little more than to take people in her lap and hug them. Yet her charisma is such that people feel great relief from their problems; thousands flock to meet her wherever she travels in the world. Satya Sai Baba, another charismatic twentieth-century Indian guru, seems to make sacred ash miraculously appear in his hand or on his portraits, by which many people claim to be healed. People thus flock to seek his blessings.

A charismatic spiritual leader has the ability to inspire what is often called "blind faith." The followers may feel that the person is divinely inspired and thus has God-given power to work miracles. Perhaps the greatest miracle is that of transforming people inwardly, so that their thoughts and lives change.

Close-up: Swami Prabhupada

During the twentieth century, the Western world has witnessed a miracle of personal transformation: Young people have given up popular Western culture to don saffron robes and take to the streets, chanting Hindu names of God and selling ancient Hindu texts. This was a manifestation of the Hare Krishna movement, now known as ISKCON (see p. 13). Its leader, Swami Prabhupada, was a seventy-year-old Indian who came to the United States in 1965 with only one US dollar and 600 copies of a Hindu text he had translated. His intense sense of mission nonetheless carried great weight. His own guru had instructed him to spread the praises of Lord Krishna, so he rose every night at midnight to work on his translations. His ambitious plan was to translate the basic scriptures from the Krishna-worship tradition of India (eventually he completed sixty of them, with commentaries), train a group of disciples, develop an organization, and spread the ancient teachings far and wide on foreign soil to bring a revolution in consciousness. How did he accomplish this miracle? His personal secretary writes,

Followers within the movement answer this question in theological terms: Prabhupada was the chosen vehicle to spread Lord Caitanya's message [of Krishna worship] throughout the world, in fulfillment of prophecies in scripture and promises to his guru. Historians and social scientists offer more mundane answers to this question: Prabhupada's success was largely dependent upon the existence of the youthful counter-culture looking for exotic alternatives to conventional society, the growing popularity of Eastern religions, a band of zealous followers who gave themselves wholeheartedly to publishing and distributing astonishing numbers of books and magazines and soliciting gifts, the Beatles' fascination with the chanting. Clearly, all of these were factors contributing to the success of the movement. But the single most important factor in the emergence and establishment of this movement was Prabhupada—his extraordinary spirituality, his scholarly productivity, his boundless compassion, his ceaseless energy, his audacious assurance, his shrewd judgment, his organizational skills.[3]

The ISKCON movement which Swami Prabhupada charismatically led has diminished in the United States after his death and schisms in its leadership, but its appeal continues elsewhere, including in Britain. There it has purchased a large manor house where tens of thousands of people attend religious festivals. The focus is on the charismatic appeal of Lord Krishna himself, often depicted as a beautiful youth luring his devotees with the music of his flute.

Revelation

Whereas Swami Prabhupada based his movement on ancient texts and the *bhakti* tradition (see p. 40) of fifteenth-century India spread by Lord Caitanya—as well as his own charismatic leadership—new religions often begin with a fresh revelation said to come from a supernatural source. Revelation takes different forms in different religions. In indigenous religions, shamans are specially trained to be "visited" by superhuman beings who reportedly speak through them while they are in trance, to help bring humans into proper relationship with the spirit powers. In Judaism and Islam, certain human recipients, such as Moses, the prophets, and Muhammad, were said to be instructed by God or God's angel in the ways of spirituality, and these messages were to be communicated to their societies. In Christianity, Jesus himself came to be considered the revelation of the divine in human history. In Indian religions, sages reported their inner realization of the underlying unity of everything that exists. And in religions which originated in East Asia, revelation meant comprehension of the laws of nature or of the social order. In every case, however, revelation means the disclosing or manifesting of something which is usually hidden.

If this information is hidden from ordinary human beings, how can they evaluate its truth? In his analysis of revelation in various religions, Christian professor Keith Ward of Oxford University takes a skeptical position:

> The model of "gods speaking", even though this is how shamans and prophets typically describe what happens, is much too literal and anthropomorphic. It fails to describe adequately the ambiguous nature of prophetic experience, the fact that most of it is erroneous and that there is no assured way of telling true from false, except with hindsight. What we have are, precisely, human insights, or alleged insights, which have come in dreams or visions, and which are felt as visions or auditions from the gods. . . . Rarely, one might think, does God find a mind which is attuned to the Divine reality in such a way as to communicate Divine purposes adequately.[4]

Followers of established religions feel that the inspired words of their prophets are the best or only true revelations, whereas founders of new religions claim that authentic new revelations have been granted to them. Acceptance of these new truth-claims is a major issue dividing followers of new religions from those of older movements.

Close-up: Joseph Smith of the Latter-Day Saints

Joseph Smith, Jr. (1805–44), founder of the Latter-Day Saints movement, claimed to have received a holy scripture which is comparable and supplementary to the Christian Bible. As a teenager who was concerned about the doctrinal differences between various Christian denominations, Smith prayed for guidance. He said his prayers were answered by visions of Jesus, God, and an angelic "personage" whose father, Mormon, had written the scripture fourteen centuries before on golden plates. Upon these plates, according to the angelic messenger, were engraved the history of Jesus's appearing to tribes in America who had come from Jerusalem long ago. Smith claimed that he was mystically led to find the plates and to translate them from some unknown language into English, whereafter "the messenger called for them, I delivered them up to him, and he has them in his charge until this day."[5] Joseph Smith's claim was said to be verified by eleven witnesses who wrote that he had shown them the plates, "and we also saw the engravings thereon, all of which has the appearance of ancient work, and of curious workmanship."[6]

Faith in Smith's teachings hinges upon belief in the miracle of the revealed golden plates. Smith claimed that his translation of the plates, *The Book of Mormon*, constitutes a supplement to the Bible, a second record of God's word. According to *The Book of Mormon*, God said, "Because you have a Bible ye need not suppose that it contains all my words; neither need ye suppose that I have not caused more to be written."[7] In *The Book of Mormon* is found the famous Sermon on the Mount, which repeats almost verbatim the version in the Authorized King James translation of the biblical book of Matthew. The explanation given for this obvious similarity with the Christian Bible is that the same words were also preached directly to inhabitants of America by a supernatural figure clothed in a white robe.

In addition to teachings similar to those in the Christian Bible, much of the scripture concerns the doctrine of life after death. The soul and body are said to be first separated and then united for physical resurrection into eternal happiness or misery. Great emphasis is thus placed on avoidance of sin, repentance, and baptism in the name of Jesus, to gain his atonement for sins. In *The Book of Mormon*, Jesus bluntly states that those who do not believe in him, and who are not baptized, will be damned.

The teachings foresee a second coming of Christ and a thousand-year reign of goodness. This transformation will follow the "latter days," in which society has become so corrupt that even the churches are defiled. According to the prophecies in *The Book of Mormon*, the Second Coming

> shall come in a day when there shall be heard of fires, and
> tempests, and vapors of smoke in foreign lands;
> And there shall also be heard of wars, rumors of wars,

and earthquakes in divers places.

Yea, it shall come in a day when there shall be great
pollutions upon the face of the earth; there shall be murders,
and robbing, and lying, and deceivings, and whoredoms, and
all manner of abominations; when there shall be many who
will say, Do this, or do that, and it mattereth not, for the
Lord will uphold such at the last day. . . . Yea, it shall come
in a day when there shall be churches built up that shall say:
Come unto me, and for your money you shall be forgiven of
your sins.⁸

With such revelations, Smith convinced many people that they were living in the latter days and should make preparations for the salvation of
their souls. The prophecies about the latter days can readily be related
to today's conditions, and the Church's emphasis on close and struc-
tured family life also has strong contemporary appeal, so Smith's message continues to spread. His Church of Jesus Christ of Latter-Day
Saints now has some 9.5 million followers, some 50,000 zealous missionaries serving voluntarily to spread the movement around the world,
and translations of *The Book of Mormon* into over eighty languages.

Millennial Expectations

In addition to the impetus of charismatic founders or compelling revelations, new religions often arise in troubled times out of the idea that
major changes will soon occur. Again and again throughout the history
of religions—and particularly during times of social chaos or oppression—there have been periods replete with millennial expectations. The
term **millennium** comes from Christianity. It refers to the expectation
that Jesus will return again to usher in a thousand-year period of goodness, as described in detail in Revelation, the last book in the Bible.
Christianity has thus spawned many millennial movements over time,
including the Latter-Day Saints. More generally, the term millennarian
is used to refer to all religious movements which anticipate the coming
of a Golden Age.

Some such movements accentuate the positive—a hopeful expectation of change for the better. This attitude characterizes New Age
groups. This amorphous spiritual trend, which has developed in the last
decades of the twentieth century, encompasses people around the world
who are questioning old structures and hoping to usher in a better time

ahead. In this movement—whose roots include Western metaphysical traditions and various Eastern religions—there is no particular theology, no founder, no institutionalized religion. Instead, the emphasis is on direct mystical experience, faith, inner transformation, surrender to the divine, spiritual healing. These topics are often purveyed through workshops by self-appointed specialists. In 1994, popular New Age author Marianne Williamson offered her own explanation of the variegated movement:

> We are an assorted group, an unlabeled group, but together in spirit, we are affecting the world in significant ways. We are turning away from a purely worldly orientation. . . . We feel a current of change, a cosmic electricity running through our veins now. However disparate our personalities and interests, we all agree on one very important point: Mankind has come to a major crossroads, at which the spirit alone can lead us toward human survival. . . . We hope to change the world into a place of grace and love. . . .
>
> From channeled entities claiming to hail from the Pleiades to fundamentalist Christians, from the prophecies of Nostradamus to visions of the Virgin Mary, from angels who whisper to a backwoods carpenter to scientific think tanks, come predictions of global shift, perhaps cataclysm, in the years ahead. . . . Should we choose to expand who we are on a fundamental level, new structures will replace the casualties of premillennial disintegration, and the next twenty years will usher in an age of light more dazzling than the world has known. . . . We're a revolution.[9]

New Age spirituality is based on the optimistic theme that although things are bad now, they may soon be better if enough people create a positive spiritual atmosphere surrounding the planet through their thoughts and prayers. However, at the dawn of the twenty-first century, optimistic references to the "New Age" are declining. Other millennial movements emphasize the negative: the expectation that things will get even worse before they become better. This idea is often coupled with belief that evil will be horribly punished, while the faithful will be saved. Such millennarian movements generally try to warn the populace of an impending apocalypse, a catastrophic end to the existing world. According to the gospel of Mark, Jesus said,

When you hear the noise of battle near at hand and the news
of battles far away, do not be alarmed. Such things are
bound to happen; but the end is still to come. For nation will
make war upon nation, kingdom upon kingdom; there will be
earthquakes in many places; there will be famines. With
these things the birth-pangs of the new age begin. . . .

Those days will bring distress such as never has been
since the beginning of the world which God created—and
will never be again. . . . [10]

Although Jesus warned again and again that the coming of the kingdom of God was very near at hand, the apocalypse did not occur at that
time in any obvious form. The biblical predictions have thus sometimes
been interpreted as metaphors. That is, some feel that biblical references
to the gathering of the faithful by angels at the time of the apocalypse
refer to the inner experience of being lifted up to the divine presence by
God's overwhelming power, and thus losing all attachment to worldly life.
Others have continued to believe literally that there will be an outward
end of the present world and that the end days are near at hand.

In societies which count their years according to the Christian calendar, such expectations abound at the beginning of the twenty-first
century. The year 2000 C.E. is widely considered to be a major turning-
point in human history. Warfare in many parts of the world, exposure of
corruption in high places, airplane crashes, climate change, droughts,
floods, earthquakes, and massive forest fires give many people the sense
that great disaster or change is looming. The occurrence of the worst El
Niño (the climate-altering warm phase of a warm-cold pattern in the
Pacific Ocean) in history in 1997/98 increased such expectations.

However, millennarian ideologies are not unique to the turn of the
twenty-first century. For instance, they were very common among Jews
in the first century during Roman oppression and again in the seven-
teenth century when Jews were being persecuted in Europe. Mircea
Eliade, an influential scholar of comparative religion, observed that
indigenous religions have long told stories about the fall of humans from
the realm of the sacred to the everyday "profane" world. This separation
from the sacred realm is accompanied by deep longing for Paradise,
longing to "live in the world as it came from the Creator's hands, fresh,
pure, and strong."[11] Living in a world of human error and chaos, people
are naturally sympathetic to predictions that a return to heaven soon
awaits, for those who are faithful and good.

Sociologists offer additional explanations for the persistence of such ideas. Because millennarians live within a belief-system which is quite at odds with that of the surrounding society, bonding among believers is very strong. Even if others reject their ideas, they can easily see that the mainstream society is unenlightened. Many already felt alienated from the mass culture; the alternative spiritual community was more appealing even though it was in the minority. By trying to warn and convince others of the impending apocalypse, members become reinforced in their own beliefs and group identity. They may develop elaborate arguments supporting their alternate view, sometimes with extensive references to scriptural passages. Even if a member has some private doubts, it seems dangerous to take chances with eternity by rejecting salvation.

Thus enfolded in their own worldview, which they have been convinced is correct, some millennarian movements have gone to bizarre extremes. Followers of the Order of the Solar Temple seem to have believed that by committing ritual suicide, they would be carried to a new world on another planet. Supporting each other in this belief, some seventy-four members of Solar Temple groups in Canada, Switzerland, and France committed suicide together between 1995 and 1997, with their bodies arranged in stars or crosses.

Close-up: Jehovah's Witnesses

One of the most firmly established new religious movements which bases its mission on apocalyptic predictions is Jehovah's Witnesses. Jehovah's Witnesses believe that we are living in a "harvest period," the end days of the present world, and should dramatically change our lives accordingly.

The movement can be traced to the 1830s, when a Baptist leader named William Miller announced that the Bible is full of secret numerical clues. According to his interpretation of scriptural passages, he wrote of his conviction that Christ would return to earth some time between March 21, 1843 and March 21, 1844. An estimated 100,000 people accepted his message and formed an informal network to anticipate the Second Coming, often leaving their mainstream Christian churches in the process. When March 21, 1844 came and went without anything notable happening, Miller hopefully submitted that Jesus would appear by October 22 of the same year. This predicted great event also failed to happen. From the ensuing confusion, two major new movements sprouted: Seventh-Day Adventists and Jehovah's Witnesses. Both continued to anticipate the end times, and Jehovah's Witnesses repeatedly set specific dates for the coming of Christ.

Charles Taze Russell was the founder of the Jehovah's Witness movement. He was a businessman who had become disillusioned with his mainstream Presbyterian Protestant Christian Church. When he encountered Miller's ideas, he became convinced that population of the whole world would be burned up in 1873 or 1874, except for Adventists. When that did not happen, Russell concluded that Christ had actually arrived but was invisibly present. Only the faithful—who came to be known as Jehovah's Witnesses—would recognize his presence. His people should thus be preparing themselves for the end of the current world, which would happen in 1878, when believers would be lifted into the air to meet Christ. Russell began publishing his views in a journal entitled *The Watchtower and Herald of Christ's Presence*. He worked so hard and had such charisma that he eventually built up a movement of over three million believers with headquarters in Brooklyn, New York. When nothing happened in 1878, Russell changed the deadline for the "harvest" of believers to 1881, and thence to 1914, then 1925, and then 1975. Each time, followers of this belief lived in a state of anticipation until the prophesied harvest failed to occur. After the failure of the 1975 prediction, approximately one million disillusioned Jehovah's Witnesses left the fold. Nonetheless, the movement is still strong.

Ramona Perez of Brooklyn, New York, is immersed in water during a mass baptism of Jehovah's Witnesses. Believers feel that baptism in the faith prepares them to be saved in the coming apocalypse.

How do people keep the faith in the face of so many failed predictions? Sociologists have observed that after the world does not end as it was expected to, believers are first disappointed, then confused. Then, partly because they yearn for salvation, they may find some way to rationalize the temporary failure and return to a state of waiting for the prophecy to come true in some fashion, perhaps soon. At the dawn of the twenty-first century, Jehovah's Witnesses are again anticipating the apocalypse.

The firm doctrines of the movement may also offer a sense of certainty amid contemporary social complexities. Jehovah's Witnesses have an extensive set of beliefs, some of which are clearly divergent from mainstream Christianity, the original source of their faith. They maintain that righteous people chosen by God will eventually inhabit the earth forever, living in a state of physical immortality in an earthly paradise which humans and animals will peacefully share. Another 144,000 of the faithful will live in heaven, ruling the earth alongside God and Jesus. Membership in The Watchtower Society is the only means of salvation; all others will perish in the battle of the final days between God's army led by Jesus and Satan's army. People should have nothing to do with Churches other than Jehovah's Witnesses, for other Churches are agents of Satan. They should also disassociate themselves as far as possible from the secular world since the final apocalypse is about to come. For instance, they should not become involved in politics, military service, displays of patriotism, use or manufacture of weapons, sports, civic organizations, pornography, belief in evolution rather than divine creation, Christmas or Easter celebrations (because these are seen as adaptations of pagan festivals), or birthday celebrations (because they are not mentioned in the Bible). Higher education is not encouraged, for it fosters secular values. Rather, families are encouraged to study the Bible and *The Watchtower* together, so that they may become strictly moral and convincing missionaries for the faith. With their strong patriarchal families, dedicated lay participation in the work of the movement, and conviction that theirs is the only way to salvation in the coming apocalypse, Jehovah's Witnesses remain one of the most popular new religious movements in the world. Their intensely committed missionaries go from door to door, attempting to engage people in conversations about the evil state of the world, the coming millennium, and their vision of salvation. *The Watchtower* is published in 110 languages and over 15 million copies of each issue are sold around the world by these missionaries.

Syncretism

Some new religious movements evolve through time without specific founders, revelations, or millennial expectations, as mixtures of previous religions. The amalgamation of otherwise different religions is called **syncretism**. This often seems to happen as religious movements disperse. As Buddhism spread into Tibet during the eighth century, it became mixed with indigenous beliefs and deities of the region, thus aiding its acceptance by the people and retaining the power of the earlier beliefs. Syncretism may also expose an underlying unity between otherwise differing faiths. For example, the ten Sikh Gurus preached to both Hindus and Muslims, whose religions are outwardly quite different. Their holy scripture incorporates the inspired writings not only of Sikh Gurus but also of Hindu and Muslim saints, finding their common ground in mystical adoration of one formless God.

Close-up: Santeria

Sometimes the juxtaposition and blending of faiths results in surprising mixtures of external aspects of the religions. Such is the case with Santeria. Now extensively practiced in the Americas, including the United States, where it is common in major cities with large Hispanic populations, the religion originated in Cuba. It was a blend of the indigenous traditions of Yoruba slaves imported from Nigeria and the Roman Catholicism which had been introduced earlier in Cuba by the sixteenth-century Spanish conquistadors. Some of the slaves were already on the run from invading tribes and colonialists in Africa when they were captured. They carried remnants of powerful cultures, including the culturally advanced kingdom of Benin. Reaching the New World, they hid their own sacred traditions from outside eyes and adopted the saints (*santos*) of the Catholic Church. But each saint was for them the replica of one of their own powerful deities, the *orisha*.

Popular Catholic stories about the saints made this dual worship possible. There is the legendary Saint Barbara, for instance. She is thought to have lived in the fourth century as daughter of a barbarian king. A virgin, she had privately given her life to Christ. Her enraged father had her imprisoned in a turret of his castle because she would not give up Christianity or marry according to his dictates. One stormy night, it is said that he drew his sword and cut off her head, whereupon he was instantly struck by a bolt of lightning. *Santeros* (practitioners of

Santeria) readily saw a similarity between her and the *orisha* Chango, who is the controller of lightning, thunder, and fire, and who is worshiped for his sheer power and control over enemies. The Catholic image of Saint Barbara typically shows her with a sword in one hand and a goblet in the other, which *santeros* identify with the mortar in which Chango prepares his magic spells. Worship of the Virgin Mary has likewise been blended with veneration of the *orisha* Oshun. She is the patron of love, marriage, and fertility and is associated with river water. When at the great St. Patrick's Cathedral in New York a mass is said for Our Lady of Charity (the Virgin Mary celebrated as patron saint of Cuba since she appeared to three shipwrecked fishermen at sea), the Cuban priest celebrating the mass openly refers to her as "Cachita," a nickname of beloved Oshun.

How similar or different are Santeria and Roman Catholicism? The Yorubas had a rich culture and strong ethics. They worshiped one God called Olodumare, source of the spiritual energy of which the whole cosmos is composed. The *orishas* are the agents of Olodumare. They control every aspect of nature and human life. If properly worshiped, they will come to the help of their followers. Specially initiated priests and

Cuban followers of Santeria, a fusion of the indigenous traditions of Yoruba slaves from Nigeria and the Roman Catholicism of the Spanish conquerors of Latin America.

priestesses help in this communication with the *orishas*, using prayers, rituals, offerings, and divination. Rather similarly, Roman Catholics worship one God, Jesus Christ, the Holy Spirit which pervades the cosmos, and the saints, whose good lives made them so divine that as God's agents in heaven they can help those on earth who beseech their aid. Catholic priests serve as intercessors between the people and God.

The greatest difference between the two traditions appears in the outer methods of worship. In Santeria, worship is overtly magical. Natural objects such as herbs, stones, and cowrie shells are used for communicating with the *orishas* and kept reverently hidden in tureens. Priests and priestesses engage in shamanic practices such as dancing and trance possession to perform services such as healing of the sick. The practice which brought criticism of *santeros* in Christian cultures is the reliance on ritual animal sacrifices for especially difficult problems. Animal sacrifice was also practiced in ancient Judaism but it is shunned by the Judeo-Christian tradition today. However, in the sacrament of Holy Communion, Christians ritually drink wine and eat bread, symbolizing the blood and body of Jesus, and they do not oppose the killing of animals for food.

Whether the traditions are similar or dissimilar, they are firmly fused in Santeria. This syncretistic mixture of Yoruba and Catholic religious traditions has now become so widespread that an estimated 100 million people in Latin America and the United States now practice Santeria, and some are now undertaking spiritual pilgrimages to Nigeria to rediscover the roots of their religion. Santeria can also be found on the Internet, with websites explaining the major tenets of the religion.

Organizing a Movement

Religious movements arise as a result of the factors discussed above—charismatic founders, revelations, millennial expectations, or syncretism. Once institutionalized, they are spread by different means. During the lifetime of Jesus, for instance, little was done to organize a formal movement. Jesus had no ecclesiastical structure, no established liturgy, no fundraising program, no buildings. His spiritual impact was direct; he healed and transformed people without any organization. It was his disciples who began development of the organization and doctrines which came to be called "Christianity." Without their efforts, it is possible that the work and teachings of Jesus would have been lost in time. But the process of institutionalizing spiritual inspiration always carries the possibility that the character of the original will be affected.

In our times, some new religious movements are managed like multinational businesses, handling large sums of money and keeping in touch with followers throughout the world by means of the latest communication technologies. Developing global-scale movements within a short period of time requires considerable managerial skill.

Close-up: Siddha Yoga

A contemporary example of careful development of a religious movement can be found in Siddha Yoga. It is based in teachings from ancient India but began to take shape as a distinct movement in the middle of the twentieth century. Its focal point was a renunciate monk named Nityananda. He did not speak much and lived very simply, wandering about dressed only in a loincloth, without regard for social comforts or conventions. Eventually he settled down near Bombay, and his fame spread as a person of extraordinary spiritual powers. By the time of his death in 1961, an informal organization had begun to form around him, as people came wanting his *darshan* (the transformational blessing of being in the presence of a God-realized being or deity). The donations of Nityananda's visitors were used to build a spiritual center, repair the local temple, spruce up the hot spring in the area, and build a school and hospital.

When Nityananda died, many of his admirers thought him irreplaceable. They sat his body upright in a meditative position and built a shrine around it. The shrine became a place of pilgrimage, for his spiritual vibrations were thought to emanate perpetually thenceforth. However, one of Nityananda's chief disciples, Swami Muktananda, claimed that before his death, the revered guru had secretly passed on his position to him. Unlike his teacher, Muktananda was trained in traditional philosophy, and had often been called on to explain his teacher's brief communications. Also unlike his teacher, he took the seat of guruship in royal fashion, rather than as part of a simple lifestyle. Because he was thought also to possess great spiritual power, his following increased, so he enlarged the ashram (spiritual community gathered around a guru) and arranged accommodations for foreign followers. In 1970, he undertook a world tour. Then in 1974, he formally established a legal institution in the United States called the Siddha Yoga Dham of America (SYDA) Foundation. By 1980 the growing foundation made its headquarters and retreat center in rural South Fallsburg, New York. It is a legal body whose work is to possess real estate, maintain a staff, cover expenses of travel, publicity, and programs, publish books, and build an archive of the teacher's public talks.

At the same time, Muktananda was turning the few words of his predecessor into a spiritual system, with theology taken from the worship of Lord Shiva. At its center is the relationship of the disciple to the guru. In this system, which he called Siddha Yoga, it is the guru's grace which awakens the sleeping spiritual power (*kundalini*) in the follower. Thereafter, one can advance toward full realization of the great Self, or Shiva—the existence, consciousness, and absolute bliss which pervade the cosmos, creating, sustaining, and dissolving everything. Muktananda felt that Nityananda had bestowed this experience on him, and that the power of his guru was working in him. He was thus able to confer immediate God-realization on people whether they were spiritually advanced or not, through the powerful *shaktipat* experience. It was effected by means such as merely touching a person on the "Third Eye" in the forehead. Previously, this form of initiation had been reserved for rare and carefully trained adepts, but Muktananda made it widely available to the public. Christina Grof, who found her emotional life shattered and uncontrollable after receiving *shaktipat* from Muktananda, recounts:

> Suddenly I felt as though I had been plugged into a high-voltage socket as I started to shake uncontrollably. My breathing fell into an automatic, rapid rhythm that seemed beyond my control, and a multitude of visions flooded my consciousness. I wept as I felt myself being born; I experienced death; I plunged into pain and ecstasy, strength and gentleness, love and fear, depths and heights. I was on an experiential roller coaster, and I knew I could no longer contain it.[12]

Because of the intensity of such experiences, Muktananda developed a weekend program of spiritual preparation, with lectures, Hindu chanting, and meditation, and then *shaktipat*. The collapsing of years of training in powerful spiritual practices into a single "intensive" weekend, with instant initiation into esoteric mystical experiences, is typical of many new manifestations of ancient spiritual movements in the West.

Many people were drawn to the shortcut to enlightenment offered by Muktananda, and thus the Siddha Yoga movement grew and flourished. Liturgically it also grew, for Muktananda instituted a daily routine of *hatha yoga* (physical postures to aid health and support spiritual realization) and chanting in Sanskrit, the language of ancient Indian spiritual texts. Crowning the devotions is recitation of a traditional Indian text encouraging veneration of one's guru.

Although Muktananda steadfastly encouraged devotion to his guru, Nityananda, none of these practices was part of his guru's informal spiritual appeal. All were part of Muktananda's increasing institutionalization of Siddha Yoga. He further built his institution by training and initiating some seventy men and women as renunciate monks and nuns to carry on the work, and developing 200 centers in the United States, where meetings are held on a regular basis to introduce people to meditation and the Siddha Yoga program. After Muktananda's death in 1982, organizational aspects of the work were further strengthened by his successor Swami Chidvilasananda. She travels extensively and uses all modern means of communication to increase the global base of Siddha Yoga. But like Muktananda, she is also a spiritual adept who can transmit *shaktipat*, as well as a capable administrator. This combination of organizational skills and recognizable spirituality seems to be central to the success of many new religious movements.

Persecution vs. Freedom of Choice?

No prophet has ever been welcomed by the prevailing religious authorities. Ensconced in its own power structure, the religious establishment is likely to regard with suspicion or hostility any reformer or person claiming a new revelation. Thus the founders of new religious movements have always been persecuted. Jesus was treated as a blasphemer—one who speaks irreverently of sacred things—by the Jewish authorities and crucified by Roman officials. For several hundred years his followers were also martyred. The Prophet Muhammad was hounded by religious authorities who were making a living from pilgrims to the Ka'ba. The nineteenth-century prophet Baha'u'llah of the universalist Baha'i faith (see Chapter 4) was tortured, banished, and imprisoned by Muslim authorities because he claimed to be a new messenger of God, whereas they regarded Muhammad as the final prophet. Despite such severe persecution, Christianity, Islam, and Baha'i grew and flourish today. And today some established religions are continuing to attack new religious movements, just as they themselves were once persecuted.

Contemporary persecution of new religious movements takes many forms. In Russia, during a brief period of religious freedom following the fall of the Soviet Union in the early 1990s, missionaries streamed into the country to offer spiritual aid to the Russian populace. Imported and new religious movements—some of which were extremist or involved in financial scams—proliferated so rapidly that the Russian Orthodox Church, which had maintained a certain power base under Soviet rule, became alarmed. Some Church officials expressed dismay at the unfair economic advantage held by foreign-funded missionary organizations. In 1997, a new law was passed recognizing "the particular role of the Orthodox Church in the history of Russia" and reserving special privileges for the Orthodox Church. Judaism, Islam, Buddhism, and certain other forms of Christianity which had been active in Russia for at least fifteen years previously were also granted protection. All other groups— and there are many—were strictly restricted, turned out of their places of worship, and forbidden to conduct religious ceremonies or to publish religious materials.

In the United States, citizens are guaranteed the right to freedom of religious choice by the First Amendment of the Constitution, because many of the initial founders of the national government were Protestants who came to the land in search of freedom from religious oppression in Europe. Nevertheless, there are those in the United States who claim that society should protect people from "false prophets" who lead their followers into danger, abuse their faith by extracting money or sexual favors from them, or pose a danger to the population. The Tokyo subway attacks by Aum Supreme Truth and mass suicides by the Order of the Solar Temple (see p. 82) are extreme examples of dangers said to be posed by contemporary new religious movements to people both inside and outside the movements.

There have also been protests that some extremist new religious movements "brainwash" their followers into submission. This claim was first advanced with reference to established religions which intimidate people by issuing dire threats of hellfire, and lure them to conversion by promising salvation. During the twentieth century, the idea spread that certain new religious movements were intentionally brainwashing their would-be converts. The method was said to be insidious: After deceptive recruiting, the movements allegedly destroyed the potential converts' identities and ability to make independent choices by surrounding them with love, cutting off their contacts with people outside the group, depriving them of sleep and food, keeping them hard at work, and numbing their minds with chanting. Then, it is said, the converts were mentally "programmed" to surrender their ego and blindly follow the new movement. Children of the converts were likewise said to be isolated from the rest of society, schooled within the group, and sometimes denied outside medical care.

These criticisms were spearheaded by the **anti-cult network,** consisting of groups such as the Cult Awareness Network and the American Family Foundation. The word **cult** is neutral, meaning a religious movement centered on worship of a particular person or deity. Critics often apply this label to all new religious movements, with the negative implication (sometimes justified) that they are temporary groupings of followers around a charismatic leader who is exploiting them for the sake of money or power. To support this claim, they have surveyed people who have left new religious movements and are therefore typically critical of them. The American Family Foundation, for instance, surveyed 308 former members of new religious movements and found that 88 percent felt that the group to which they had belonged was harmful for its members; 72 percent said that group pressure made it difficult to leave the movement.

Mental health professionals have likewise issued warnings about the psychological damage done by new religious movements. For example, Dr. Marc Galanter of New York University Medical School interviewed thousands of members of new religious movements centered on charismatic leaders. He concluded that the most likely converts were people who already felt lonely and isolated from the mass culture. In the new movement, they were given a feeling of belonging. In the case of apocalyptic groups, they were encouraged in feeling a "shared paranoia" and thus were bonded to the group to such an extent that they were willing "to die together rather than to submit to evil outside forces."[13]

In the 1970s, when concern over new religious movements was mounting in the United States, controversial **deprogramming** techniques were developed to wrest converts away from the religious groups they had joined. The argument was that converts were so brainwashed that they had lost their freedom of thought and therefore could not have been rational when choosing to join such movements. Deprogrammers hired by anxious families thus used tactics such as kidnaping young people who had joined new movements. They then subjected their captives to shock treatment, using methods such as destroying pictures of the movements' founders before them and grilling them with questions which would lead them to doubt the movement. Such forceful tactics were arguably themselves illegal and have been condemned by the National Council of Churches.

Various arguments have been advanced in favor of freedom of choice for new religious movements, so long as they are not doing anything illegal. While some new religious movements may be dangerous or exploitative for their followers, so may versions of established religions. New religious movements are as varied as older religions, and they protest against being lumped together categorically as "cults." In the United States, the Civil Liberties Union argues that the First Amendment protects all religions as being equally good or bad. The National Council of Churches supports freedom of religious choice and points out that all major religions began as new religious movements. Dean Kelley, advisor to the National Council of Churches on religious liberties, says,

> People ought to be free to follow whatever religion they want
> without being forcibly rescued. The anticult cults say that
> [new religious movements] are unnatural, but it is ironic
> that as the new religions progress, they become larger and
> more numerous and become pillars of the community, like
> the Mormons.[14]

Close-up: The Unification Church

An interesting case of the response of a new religious movement to persecution is provided by the Unification Church. Its followers are often called "Moonies" by the press. The label refers to the group's controversial founder, Reverend Sun Myung Moon, but also derisively suggests that the followers are deranged ("moonstruck"). Reverend Moon is a former Christian Sunday-school teacher from Korea who claims that Jesus came to him in a vision. According to Moon, Jesus told him that his crucifixion was a mistake, for his mission was left unfinished, and that it was up to Reverend Moon to complete his task and thus establish the kingdom of God on earth. Moon elaborated this idea into a unique theology based on his own interpretation of the Biblical story of Adam and Eve. He reasoned that their "false love" had been perpetuated generation to generation throughout the human race. He, Reverend Moon, had come as the new Messiah to "engraft" followers onto a new lineage of self-sacrificial love. According to Moon, Jesus should have done so, but he never married.

Spreading this Moon-centric message was difficult from the start. Before the Second World War, even mainstream Christians in Korea were not able to practice their religion openly, for they were living under

Japanese oppression. Moon was put in jail by the Japanese as a Korean nationalist. After the war, he tried to interest Christian authorities in adopting his theology, in order to help unify the Christian denominations. But they would have nothing to do with him and his unusual ideas. Thence he was called by God, he claims, to carry on his missionary activities in communist North Korea, where religion was being suppressed. There he was imprisoned and tortured so badly that his apparently dead body was thrown outside in a snowdrift. Some followers found him and nursed him back to health. He began preaching publicly again, and again was arrested and sent to an extermination camp, where most prisoners soon died from overwork or execution. UN forces liberated the prison the night before he was to be executed. With a few of his former followers, he traveled to South Korea and built the first Unification Church out of army ration boxes.

When professors and students from a Christian women's university began to attend his classes, the university president ordered them to leave the controversial movement or be expelled from the university. At the same time, the press began printing rumors that those who spent long nights with Reverend Moon were actually engaging in sexual orgies and that Moon was in fact a North Korean spy. He was again thrown in jail twice, on unsubstantiated charges.

In the 1970s, Reverend Moon launched an appeal to young people in the United States who were disillusioned with the excessive materialism of the culture and were searching for alternative, altruistic lifestyles. He told them he had come to revive Christian ideals, for "Unless we ignite a spiritual revival in this country, the future of the world will be very bleak."[15] The Unification Church staged large rallies emphasizing moral renewal, and its membership quickly swelled. Young people from middle-class families set aside their careers, gave away their worldly goods, left their girlfriends and boyfriends, abandoned the mainstream culture's materialism and hedonism, and fell into line with the ascetic, self-sacrificing religious path set forth by Reverend Moon. They were taught to rise early in the morning to pray and meditate, to fast frequently, to shun extramarital sex, and to practice love for others of all cultural backgrounds. The most dedicated were sent as missionaries to foreign countries, to win converts. Their alarmed parents accused the Unification Church of brainwashing their children. Some were captured from the movement and deprogrammed, and all press accounts of the movement were extremely negative. Liberals were suspicious of Reverend Moon's anti-communist activities and capitalist connections;

conservative Christians could not tolerate his theology, which seemed blasphemous in its assertions that Jesus was wrong. Since the United States was founded on principles of religious freedom, Reverend Moon could not be convicted for blasphemy. But he was eventually prosecuted and jailed for a civil offense: tax evasion. The amount of money in dispute was not large, and some mainstream Christian churches joined his appeal. They apparently recognized that his trial involved a gray area in personal use of monies gathered in the name of a nonprofit organization—a legal issue which might apply to them as well—and argued that the right of freedom of religion was under attack.

Reverend Moon's persistent work and emphasis on family values has led to an international movement whose most visible manifestation is huge wedding ceremonies in which hundreds of thousands—or even millions—of couples are married or renew their marriage vows under the "Blessing" of Reverend and Mrs. Moon. The huge 1997 "Blessing Ceremony" was officially welcomed by the city of Washington, D.C., where 28,000 couples were "blessed" in RFK Stadium, representing 40 million couples in 185 countries who received the blessing by satellite and video links.

Having raised money by door-to-door sales and large-scale entrepreneurial ventures, Unification members fund expensive conferences of scholars, scientists, former heads of state, and media specialists, all designed to bring spiritual values into society, and also to glorify and legitimize the self-proclaimed roles of Reverend and Mrs. Moon as the True Parents of humanity. The Church itself is quite small, encompassing only perhaps a hundred thousand active followers, but its outreach programs touch many more people who do not agree with Reverend Moon's theology or consider him their Messiah.

Reverend Moon's determined rise from severe persecution to a degree of official welcome within his lifetime offers an unusual opportunity to study the processes by which some persecuted new religious movements persist and may even join the mainstream. Sociologists of religion have discerned three stages in persecution, which fledgling religious movements might actually turn to their own advantage to gain sympathy. The first is **self-stigmatization**, meaning that organizations which are branded as negative or deviant adopt that identity as a way of defining their mission to save the rest of society. Second is **dramatization**, by which the negatively labeled movement, instead of hiding, openly tries to carry out its claims to legitimacy and special purpose. The third is **criminalization**, by which societies actively retaliate, justifying repression by declaring the movement not only abnormal but illegal.[16] Self-stigmatization and dramatization are evident in Moon's talks. In a 1996 speech, he said,

> You have to realize that Reverend Moon overcame death hundreds of times in order to find this path. Reverend Moon is the person who brought God to tears hundreds of times. No one in history has loved God more than the Reverend Moon has. That is why even if the world tries to destroy me, the Reverend Moon will never perish. . . . If you step into the realm of the truth Reverend Moon teaches, you also will gain God's protection.[17]

Thus the movement continues, but now with a new name—The Family Federation for World Peace—to disassociate it from its stigmatized past.

After the Founder Dies

Even if they survive persecution, new religious movements face another crisis when their founders die. If the central figure has been the charismatic focus of the religion, one might imagine that the movement would wither away after his or her death. Often this is the case. But many movements have survived this crisis of leadership and grown even larger after the founder dies. This seems possible when there are successive leaders who are sufficiently determined to carry on the work or to glorify the founder's name. Successorship is a major stumbling-block, however, especially when the founder dies without making clear his preference. If followers will not accept the new leader who is chosen or who asserts his or her authority, then the movement might splinter into rival groups or else simply fall apart. During the lifetime of Joseph Smith, Jr., founder of the Latter-Day Saints, ten different factions challenged his leadership and formed splinter groups. He had at various times named seven different people as his successor, so there were further splits after he died suddenly in 1844 without leaving any clear instructions as to which one should step into his shoes. By the turn of the twenty-first century, schisms have led to some 200 different denominations tracing their roots to Smith, with the 9.5-million-member Church of Jesus Christ of Latter-Day Saints being the largest.

Sociologist Max Weber suggested that not only accepted successorship but also the **routinization of charisma** is necessary for the continuation of a new religious movement after its charismatic leader dies. That is, established theology and managerial organizations replace the original spiritual drive of the founder. When this happens, new religious movements begin to look more and more like the mainstream religions which they once critiqued. However, as we have seen, not all new religious movements stem from charismatic founders. Some, like Santeria, have no specific founder at all. And some, such as Pentecostalism, maintain spiritually dynamic qualities over long periods.

Close-up: The Celestial Church of Christ

In 1985, the charismatic founder of the West African-based Celestial Church of Christ, Samuel Oschoffa, died suddenly. However, his mission has continued so successfully that it has become the largest Church in West Africa; in its global outreach, moreover, it has founded eight churches in Washington D.C. alone. Professor Jacob Olupona suggests that this has been possible because charismatic leadership and institutional power have long been united in the Church.[18]

The founder's mystical experiences and charismatic power are clearly central to the movement's appeal. Working as a carpenter, Oschoffa received his spiritual calling when he went by canoe to buy planks from a village. An eclipse occurred on the way, and simultaneously a peacock, a bird, and a snake appeared. Terrified, the canoe's owner fled, leaving Oschoffa in an unfamiliar wilderness with only snakes, crocodiles, and birds around him. For three months he saw no humans but constantly heard a voice saying "Grace to God." When at last he made his way to a village, he brought dead children back to life by the mere touch of his hand. Then, according to his account,

> As I was praying at home, I saw a very bright light like that
> of a car's headlights and further in the light I saw an angel
> with two bright shining crystal eyes. The angel called me and
> said, "The son of man, we want to send you into the world
> because so many believers are worshipping gods and
> Mammon and because of this we are sending you into the
> world to warn them to worship only Christ. And I am giving
> you powers to wake the dead, and perform all types of
> miracles in the name of God.[19]

With this and other visionary experiences and healings by Oschoffa and some of his converts, the nucleus of a new Church was formed. Most of the converts had been Roman Catholics. At first the majority were poor village peasants, fishermen, and tradesmen; later the movement grew very rapidly in urban areas, gaining middle-class supporters. Initially the movement was mostly charismatic, without any particular structure or priests, and driven by Oschoffa's personal appeal. But to sustain the movement—to "routinize its charisma"—Oschoffa organized his follow-ers into an elaborate hierarchy of thirteen ranks, with himself at the top as pastor-founder. Although rising through the ranks was encouraged, all members were considered capable of receiving revelations during the worship services, and their visions were recorded, interpreted by the leaders, and acted upon. Older women particularly were seen as having special gifts of prophecy.

Each church was to be governed by a council of thirty members whom the pastor-founder appointed. Above them was a general commit-tee, a board of trustees to handle property matters, and a decision-mak-ing group, with the pastor-founder presiding over all these groups and exercising final authority. Oschoffa thus maintained the supreme man-agerial function and also the supreme spiritual function as prophet. However, to provide for his orderly succession, he arranged a constitu-tion stating that whomever he would appoint to succeed him after death would also have charismatic authority. Thus when he died suddenly in 1985, the congregations already had visionary vigor themselves and they had been prepared to accept the spiritual authority of a new pastor, Oschoffa's second-in-command A. A. Bada, although no one but Oschoffa would ever be pastor-founder. The Church continues to grow under Pastor Bada, with no major splits or changes in mission, and now parish-es have sprung up on nearly every continent, including a parish in Russia.

Conclusion

At the turn of the century, new religions as well as old are showing con-siderable vigor. In this chapter, we have looked at processes by which new movements are created, spread, and organized into abiding institu-tions. Some, but not all, are centered on charismatic leaders such as Swami Prabhupada, founder of ISKCON, or new revelations, such as the golden plates which Joseph Smith, Jr., founder of the Latter-Day Saints, claimed to have found. Some new religious movements arise amidst expectations that we are about to witness the end of the world as we know it, an idea which is common in our times in both optimistic and pessimistic versions. Many such movements, including Jehovah's Witnesses, stem from Christian millennial beliefs. A third general way in which new religions arise is through syncretistic combinations of previous religions, as in the case of Santeria.

These factors are rarely sufficient in themselves to guarantee a movement long life, particularly if a founder dies suddenly without having anointed a successor. Developing an organizational structure, rather like building a business, is often crucial to a religion's growth, though as we saw in the case of Siddha Yoga (see p. 88), this process can fundamentally alter the character of the original.

A major issue associated with the spread of new religious movements is their non-acceptance and sometimes persecution by segments of society, including established religions. In the twentieth century, attempts to suppress new religious movements were justified on the grounds that they were harmful for their members or for society. Those opposed to this approach support freedom of religious choice as an individual right. Ultimately, the argument hinges on whether followers who exercise their choice can do so in an informed way and without undue coercion.

Once the founder dies, means have to be found to perpetuate the early vibrancy of new religious movements and to assure their future continuation. Since the two activities may be at odds with each other, this paradoxical process can be called "the routinization of charisma." Those new movements which survive the death of their founder and show continued growth may eventually gain some social legitimacy as established religions themselves. We can expect these processes to continue apace into the twenty-first century, with many new movements being woven into the variegated spiritual fabric of the planet.

A great variety of religions are being practiced at the turn of the twenty-first century. As we have seen, many are heading vigorously in quite different directions. Even within a single religion, groups are following paths that diverge from the original message—groups which might be as different as feminist Jews and ultra-Orthodox Jews. Misunderstandings, intolerance, and competition between the various religions, and even versions of the same religion, have histori-

cally been significant sources of conflict. The Christian Church, for instance, has split over time into 21,000 different denominations, some of them quite antagonistic toward each other, despite their founder's teachings to love one's neighbor.

Now that cultures are mixing to an unprecedented extent, the potential for conflictual relationships has increased. But at the same time, many efforts are being made to enhance harmony between people on different religious paths. In this chapter we will first consider the question of whether or not religions are actually teaching the same thing: Are there some underlying similarities which, if recognized, could help to ease tensions between religions? Then we will look at two rather new religions—Sikhism and Baha'i—which explicitly try to encourage universal acceptance of all religions. Finally, we will examine the current efforts of the interfaith movement, whose aim is to draw humans together, rather than to separate them, as they reach toward the sacred.

Are Religions the Same or Different?

The question of the degree of sameness or difference between religions can be approached from many angles. Conclusions depend to a great extent on what aspect of religions we are viewing—be it their rituals, geographic location, founding period, doctrines, or ethics. We must also take into account the fact that each religion is complex, continually evolving, and understood in different ways by its own practitioners. Comparisons among religions must therefore be drawn on the level of broad generalizations.

If we look at outer rituals, we see that religious practices are quite dissimilar. Some religions assert that the head should be covered in holy places; some insist that it should be bared. Some assert that one should never cut one's hair since it was given by the divine; others have established monastic disciplines in which the head is to be totally shaved, for detachment from worldliness. Some have women clergy; some strictly limit women's participation. Some approach the divine offering flowers, fruits, lights, and incense; some offer live animals for sacrifice. Some worship standing; some sit crosslegged. Some maintain sober stillness before the divine; others dance and shout and fall down when they feel the presence of spiritual power.

Scholars of comparative religion once categorized faiths by their geographic location—"Eastern" vs. "Western" religions—in order to make generalizations about their similarities and differences. However, geographical distinctions are no longer useful, for as we have seen, many religions have spread around the world and are fervently practiced far from their place of origin. And if Hinduism, for instance, is assigned to a single category—"Eastern" or "Indian" religion—the vast range of practices and philosophies included in Sanatana Dharma are incorrectly and unhelpfully lumped together.

Some analysts have categorized religions on the basis of when they arose historically. According to this system, during the so-called Pre-Axial Age, ancient religions such as Sanatana Dharma and indigenous religions saw this world as suffused with the sacred. A major shift occurred during the **Axial Age**, the extremely fertile period between the eighth and fifth centuries B.C.E., in which lived many great teachers of spirituality, including Buddha, Confucius, Zarathustra, Jewish prophets, and the ancient Greek philosophers. These teachers postulated and described a sharp distinction between the worldly reality and the transcendent invisible reality. The "other world" was seen as being of a higher moral order, one to which all people of this world should aspire. The later-arising Post-Axial religions such as Christianity and Islam continued and developed this theme. However, this characterization of religions according to the period in which they originated does not hold true in all cases in the past and certainly cannot be applied to the present, when new religions as different as Neo-paganism and Jehovah's Witnesses have emerged.

During the twentieth century, scholars of comparative religion also made many efforts to analyze the extent to which religions are similar or different in doctrines. Some have concluded that religions are irreconcilably different in this regard. A basic difference seems to lie in the concept of ultimate reality. **Theistic** religions such as Christianity, Judaism, and Islam perceive a personal supreme deity or deities; nontheistic religions such as Buddhism do not speak of a creator of the cosmos but rather of nonpersonal processes such as *karma* by which life is governed. This division between religions is not utterly clear-cut, for there are theistic versions of Buddhism, and there have been Christian, Jewish, and Muslim mystics who perceive a nonpersonal ultimate reality. Nevertheless, it is difficult to say that anything in Buddhism corresponds exactly to what Christians and Jews call "God," and what Muslims call "Allah."

This fundamental doctrinal difference leads to different answers to the basic questions in life. Take the problem of suffering, for instance. For Buddhists, the existence of suffering in the world is a given fact of life. The point of spiritual practice is at last to transcend the suffering of the cycle of births and deaths. For Christians, who generally believe in a loving God who is creating and controlling everything, it is very hard to understand why this God would make good people suffer. According to Christian theology which developed from the teachings of the apostle Paul, the answer to this puzzle is the fall—the biblical story that the first humans did not suffer until they disobeyed God and thus were banished from the paradise which God had originally created. In its modern interpretation, the story of Adam and Eve is a myth illustrating that sin and suffering arose from free human choice, which has taken humanity away from God's plan. In either Christian interpretation, only through acceptance of Jesus as the savior who suffered and was crucified to redeem all humanity can one be cleansed of this flawed condition and transformed by the power of the Holy Spirit to experience inexplicable inner peace and joy.

At the level of ethics, it could be said that all religions teach the same basic human values. In some way, all faiths urge people to be more loving, altruistic, morally upright, courageously truthful. The "Universal Rule" apears in some form in every religion (see box). In Sikh scripture, we humans are said to be beset by five "enemies" which hound us from within: lust, anger, greed, ignorance, and egotism. How to overcome these negative tendencies? Methods differ, but it can be argued that the goal of escaping from our inner evils is the same in all religions. Jesus calls, "Leave everything and follow me, for I will take you to my Father's kingdom, where you will find eternal life,"[1] whereas Buddha says,

Check your mind.
Be on your guard.
Pull yourself out
as an elephant from mud.[2]

Beyond doctrines, ethics, and spiritual practices, many contemporary scholars are coming to the conclusion that there is an underlying experiential unity among religions. Wilfred Cantwell Smith, for instance, posits that all religions share a common source from which their revelations have come. Christian theologian John Hick proposes that the various religions are culturally different responses to the same one reality. Muslim scholar Frithjof Schuon proposes a common mystical ground underlying all religions, which can be experienced only through inner enlightenment, not through scholarly analyses. Discussing the difference between mysticism and philosophy, W.T. Stace explains,

Mystical experience, *during* the experience, is wholly
unconceptualizable and therefore wholly unspeakable. This
must be so. You cannot have a concept of anything *within*
the undifferentiated unity because there are no separate
items to be conceptualized... But afterwards when the
experience is remembered the matter is quite different. For
we are then in our ordinary sensory-intellectual
consciousness.[3]

Because religions can at the same time be said to be similar and also different, and also because the boundaries perceived between religions may be sources of violence, Professor Johan Galtung, founder of the International Peace Research Institute, has developed a cross-religious typology claiming to show that these boundaries do not exist for all practitioners of a faith. He suggest that religious experience can be characterized by its "heat." At the center is the intensely hot core of the *mysterium tremendum*, the direct mystical experience of the supernatural Other to which Stace pointed. Here there is only oneness of experience, whether the person experiencing the "great mystery" comes from East or West, ancient or postmodern times. Here the barriers used to delineate religious organizations have no meaning.

The Universal Rule

Scholars of comparative religions have discovered that one central ethical teaching is found in almost identical form in all major religions:

"This is the sum of duty: Do nothing unto others which would cause you pain if it were done to you"—Hinduism (Mahabharata 5:1517)

"In happiness and suffering, in joy and grief, we should regard all creatures as we regard our own self."—Jainism (Lord Mahavir)

"Hurt not others in ways that you yourself would find hurtful."—Buddhism (Udana-Varga, 5:18)

"Do not unto others what you would not have them do unto you."—Confucianism (Analects of Confucius 15:23)

"That nature only is good when it shall not do unto another whatever is not good for its own self."—Zoroastrianism (Dadistan-i-Dinik, 94:5)

"What is hateful to you, do not do to your fellow human being. That is the law; all the rest is commentary."—Judaism (Talmud, Shabbat 31a)

"Always treat others as you would like them to treat you: That is the Law and the prophets."—Christianity (Matthew 7:12)

"No one of you is a believer until he desires for his brother that which he desires for himself."—Islam (Sunnah)

"Do not create enmity with anyone, for God is within everyone."—Sikhism (Guru Granth Sahib 259)

"The foundation is respect for all life."—Native American (The Great Law of Peace)

[adapted from compilation by the Temple of Understanding]

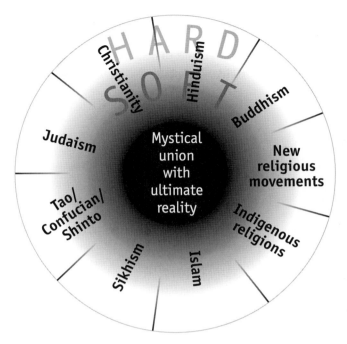

A diagram illustrating "hard" and "soft" religious beliefs. The circle's outer edge symbolizes irreconcilable differences, of either practice or doctrine, between the world's religions. The dividing lines become fainter toward the center, showing how people can set aside sectarian differences and share a common spirituality. The central core stands for the direct mystical experience, which transcends individual belief-systems.

Beyond this illuminated core of religion, Galtung posits sectors like slices of a pie, which carry the names of separate religions. They also differ from the center outward, as if in two concentric circles. The circle nearest the core, and therefore the "warmest," encompasses what Galtung calls **soft religion**. Here, explains Galtung, a Buddhist and a Christian will not meet as people of different religions with irreconcilable differences, but as fellow human beings. No formidable boundary wall stands between them. Indeed, in our times, many Christians are exploring and learning from Buddhist teachings and practicing their meditation techniques.

In the outer ring of religious experience, one would see a great difference between Christianity and Buddhism, between Islam and Sanatana Dharma, between Santeria and Jehovah's Witnesses. This hard outer ring, which exists in all religions, represents faith as an exclusive claim to truth, a sense of being chosen to carry that exclusive truth to the world in order to save everyone, of being superior to other religious paths. Here even violent suppression of other religions may be justified.

Universalist Religions

It is possible to argue that hard boundaries between religions were not so much established by their founders, as developed over time by the ensuing religious institutions, to advance their own interests. Nowhere is Jesus or Muhammad quoted as having urged hatred. But in the institutionalized divisions which developed to promote their mission, some of their followers fight even among themselves, as well as against people of other religions. In contrast to the exclusive feeling of some that their religion has the only claim to truth, two of the latest major world religions to arise—Sikhism and Baha'i—explicitly attempt to transcend religious boundaries. They do so in different ways: Sikhs are enjoined to see all humans as one, irrespective of their religions, whereas Baha'is have a vision of a single global religion.

Sikhism

Sikhism is rooted in the mystical experience of North Indian saints, both Hindu and Muslim, whose writings are included along with those of the Sikh Gurus in the Sikh scripture, the Guru Granth Sahib, without sectarian designations. This is highly unusual, for under the rule of Mughal Muslim emperors, Muslims and Hindus had become political enemies. Guru Nanak, the First Sikh Guru, reportedly disappeared into a river at the end of the fifteenth century, and had what was apparently an experience of profound enlightenment. Upon emerging, he said, "There is neither Hindu nor Muslim, so whose path shall I follow? I shall follow God's path. God is neither Hindu nor Muslim. . . ."[4]

Guru Nanak traveled far and wide, from the Himalayas in the north to Sri Lanka in the south, and as far west as Mecca, dressed as a Muslim pilgrim, with verses from the Qur'an embroidered on his robe. He confronted both Hindu and Muslim religious figures with the difference between their outer show of piety and their inner spiritual poverty, while affirming the essential truths of each religion. The path delineated by Guru Nanak was theologically uncomplicated and practical: One should work hard to support oneself, share with others from one's own honest earnings, and always remember God by reciting God's name. His path was rooted in mystical experience of God and a love for God which knows no sectarian boundaries.

Ultimately there were ten Sikh Gurus, all of whom were mystics around whom miracles were reportedly commonplace, and who emphasized the underlying truths of religion rather than external rituals. The Fifth Sikh Guru was tortured to death by the Mughal ruler, but yet he reportedly remained firm in his faith and love for God, and harbored no rancor against Muslims. The Ninth Sikh Guru gave up his life to protect freedom of religion for the Hindus. The Tenth Sikh Guru, Guru Gobind Singh (1661–1708), trained his Sikhs to offer aid to anyone who was weak and oppressed, and to stand firm against religious tyranny. He said,

> Same are the temple and the mosque
> And same are the forms of worship therein.
> All human beings are one though apparently many,
> Realize, therefore, the essential unity of mankind.[5]

Sikhs never felt they had a mandate to convert people away from other religions, so the universal movement begun by the Sikh Gurus has remained confined mostly to India and to Indians living abroad. Even though Sikhism is the fifth largest world religion, thus far the 20 million Sikhs are mostly Indians. Sikhism has also been politicized during the twentieth century. In efforts to separate the Sikhs' homeland from the central Indian government, some Sikhs developed an exclusivist identity which, it can be argued, was not consonant with their Gurus' universalist teachings (see p. 85). Their revered scripture, the Guru Granth Sahib, has undergone several rather clumsy translations into English but is generally unknown outside Sikhism.

Baha'i

By contrast, the Baha'i faith has a self-concious mission to the world. Its main founder was Baha'u'llah (1817–92) of Iran. He announced most of his revelations from exile or during imprisonment by Muslim political authorities who could not tolerate his claim to prophethood, for Muslims regarded Muhammad as the Seal of the Prophets. Though oppressed, Baha'u'llah taught appreciation for all faiths. "The religion of God is for love and unity," he said. "Make it not the cause of enmity and dissension."[6] Mere humans cannot comprehend God's infinite nature

ART FOCUS

Baha'i: Spiritual Principles in Contemporary Architecture

BAHA'IS AROUND THE WORLD take great pride in having built seven temples of striking modern design. They have been constructed out of the voluntary contributions of Baha'is everywhere, symbolizing their global vision of a future universal religion which respects but transcends older faiths. The first of these temples was a tall domed structure built in Wilmette, Illinois, followed by temples in Uganda, Australia, Germany, Panama, Western Samoa, and India. The temple completed in 1986 in New Delhi has been hailed as one of the greatest accomplishments of twentieth-century architecture.

The Baha'i House of Worship in New Delhi was conceived as a symbol which would somehow be familiar to the people of India as part of their spiritual heritage but yet not point to any one religious tradition. The symbol it depicts in huge and abstract form is that of a lotus flower floating on a pond. Fariburz Sahba, architect of the temple, explains:

> The lotus flower is rooted in slime and yet speaks of a world of purity because it floats on the surface in the utmost purity and grace and remains untainted in the midst of filth. The loveliness and immaculacy of this flower, which sparkles everywhere like a star on the waters of India, has made it a symbol of spirituality and beauty in the mythology of all the religions of India.[7]

In ancient Hindu scriptures, the lotus symbolizes divine birth, the first living thing to appear out of the chaotic primordial waters. The subtle centers of spiritual energy within a human being are also depicted as unfolding lotus blossoms. Buddhist artists used the same symbols, picturing Buddha and the Boddhisattva Avalokiteswara as seated or standing in meditation upon an open lotus. Lotus designs are found in Muslim architecture as well.

The architect determined that the lotus should be like a temple of light, just as Buddhists bow to the "Jewel in the heart of the lotus," the light present within everything. Effects of light and water are the only design elements; as in all Baha'i temples, there are no statues, no representations of the divine.

Baha'is also concern themselves with environmental preservation, so no environmentally costly air-conditioning is provided inside the temple. Even in the heat of Delhi's summer, which often reaches 113°F (45°C), the interior temperature is lowered by air drawn by fans and natural convection across the surrounding ponds and the cool basement and up through the central "bud."

The unusual building rises 112 feet (34 meters) high from an expansive garden and can be seen from far away, rising like a vision of unearthly beauty above the polluted city streets and bazaars. The visionary design has led to one odd outcome, however: interior accoustics are quite scrambled. Sounds from one point echo again and again off the other angled surfaces, overlapping and covering sounds made later. Fortunately, the temple was conceived as a place of prayer, not of sermons and lectures, so the fact that speeches can barely be understood becomes part of the spiritual atmosphere of the place. Singing takes on serendipitous overtones as the echoes multiply and overlap, lending even the simplest songs an otherworldly quality.

The Baha'i House of Worship in New Delhi is designed to resemble a lotus flower, without reference to any particular religion.

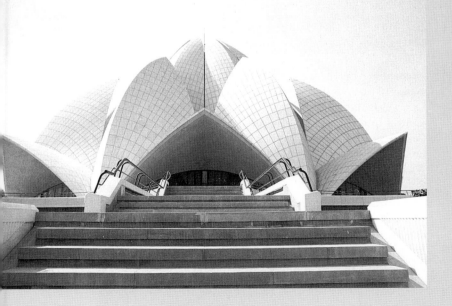

with their limited minds. Instead, God has become known through divine messengers, the founders of the world's great religions. All are manifestations of God, channels for helping humanity to understand God's will. Humanity has been maturing, like a child growing in the ability to grasp complex ideas. Each time a divine messenger appeared, the message was given at levels appropriate to humanity's degree of maturity. Baha'u'llah proclaimed that the revelations given to him are the most advanced and most appropriate for this time period. His message contains the same truth-claims as those from the earlier revelations, but with some new features which he said humanity is now ready to grasp.

The concept which Baha'is feel is new in their faith is that of oneness—oneness of all humans, oneness of the source of all religions, and oneness of all the prophets. By implementing this vision, they feel, humans now have for the first time the opportunity to unite for the sake of world peace, universal social justice, and harmoniously ordered society. Through careful arrangement for successorship, central organization, and proselytizing activities, the Baha'is have grown to five million members spread around the world. In their cultural diversity, they try to provide within their own faith a model for a "new world order" of harmonious cooperation between people of diverse backgrounds.

The Interfaith Movement

In addition to such universalist religious ideologies, there are many efforts afoot to open lines of communication between people of different religions. Harvard professor Diana Eck, former chair of the World Council of Churches, identifies three basic ways in which religions may relate to one another. One of these is **exclusivism**, the idea that one's own way is the only true way. This feeling is not trivial, for deep belief is central to religious faith. However, if this belief is mirrored by its rigid corollary—"Therefore all other religions are false and cannot be tolerated"—we will see a hardening of religious boundaries, schisms, and conflicts. These processes go on within, as well as between, religions.

According to Eck's analysis, a second form of interrelationship is **inclusivism**. This is the idea that there should be a single world religion, or that one's own religion is sufficiently spacious to accommodate all others. In this approach, the dissimilarities between religions are disregarded in favor of generalized unity.

A third approach, which Eck favors, is what she calls pluralism. In this, one keeps one's own religion and yet at the same time maintains a curious, friendly, and respectful stance toward the beliefs and practices of people of other faiths.

To transcend exclusivism and move toward a more pluralistic relationship between religions has been the goal of the **interfaith** movement. Its major impetus in the twentieth century originated in the Christian ecumenical movement. This is the effort to transcend the doctrinal and organizational differences between Christians and bring some kind of unity back to what was once a single religious movement begun by Jesus and his immediate disciples. A major step in this direction was taken in 1948, with the formation of the World Council of Churches, composed of representatives from many major Christian denominations. The Roman Catholic Church has remained aloof from the W.C.C., for the Vatican considers itself the one authentic bearer of the Christian lineage, but Catholic theologians are nonetheless individually active in exploring ecumenical themes.

Interfaith Dialogue

In addition to intra-Church attempts to heal old wounds, the twentieth century has seen many efforts at dialogue between representatives of different faiths. Jewish–Christian dialogue, for instance, seeks to take a fresh look at the old hatreds between these two historically related faiths and perhaps rediscover their areas of commonality.

The twentieth century also saw a spate of interfaith conferences, convened to promote interfaith harmony. The first major assembly of this kind occured in Chicago in 1893, as the Parliament of the World's Religions. Held before modern transportation and communication systems had shrunk the globe, the conference was an unprecedented display of cultural as well as religious differences. For delegates from the United States, the hero of the conference was Swami Vivekananda from India. Dressed in traditional Indian clothing, it was he who brought Eastern religions to the attention of the West and made these remarks at the conclusion of the historic conference:

> If the Parliament of Religions has shown anything to the
> world it is this: It has proved to the world that holiness,
> purity, and charity are not the exclusive possessions of any
> church in the world, and that every system has produced
> men and women of the most exalted character. In the face of
> this evidence, if anybody dreams of the exclusive survival of

his own religion and the destruction of others, I pity him from the bottom of my heart.[8]

Hopefulness about the harmonizing potential of interfaith meetings led to the creation of permanent committees to coordinate future events and other bridge-building exercises. These groups became large organizations, each with its own officers, membership, and funds. Ironically they began to compete for power in the interfaith arena, just as religious organizations have been adversaries in the competition for saving souls. Fighting has broken out even within these interfaith groups. One unfortunate example of this downside of the interfaith movement was the 1995 global meeting of one of the oldest such organizations, the World Conference on Religion and Peace. Held in a beautiful setting on a lake in north Italy, the conference degenerated into power struggles so irreconcilable that the final outcome was the appointment of twenty-eight presidents of the organization. It is a sad irony that many members of this organization are trying to help bring peace and reconciliation in areas of inter-religious strife, such as former Yugoslavia.

Nonetheless, hopefulness about this approach persists. The 1993 centennial of the Chicago Parliament of the World's Religions was open to the general public and some 8,700 people attended, from 125 religions, with thousands more being turned away for lack of space. The participants were treated to a smorgasbord sampling of hundreds of spiritual experiences and teachings from a great variety of religions. Christian monk Brother Wayne Teasdale praised the event as the heralding of a Second Axial Age in which "nationalism and fanaticism will evaporate before the human family's discovery of a more universal identity." He calls the parliament "a transcendent moment in history animated by a spirit of genuine openness, mutual listening, and respect."[9]

However, the parliament included an elite meeting of some 300 of the world's most renowned religious leaders. Delegates were told to discuss a document on global ethics which they could not change, and the meetings of this august body disintegrated into shouting over parliamentary procedures. One could conclude that individuals may be freer to be open-minded than institutionalized religions and their leaders, who are committed to propagating their own way.

There are also many scholarly conferences devoted to plumbing the apparent differences between religions and to finding some common ground, or at least an appreciation of the differences. Thus, scholars of different religions convene internationally to explore differences in basic principles, such as their concepts of ultimate reality or explanations of the existence of evil. In such nonthreatening settings, differences can be explored without any sense of competition, and members of different faiths, even if they do not agree, may at least become more sensitive toward each other.

The latest manifestation of the contemporary interfaith movement is the idea that there should be a permanent group of religious leaders meeting to give advice to the United Nations or the world at large on global problems. This idea is being promoted in different forms by at least four different organizations. One of these, the United Religious Initiative, was organized by Episcopal bishop William Swing of California with the noble ideal of developing an ongoing body of high-ranking religious representatives who would meet with each other daily. The plan, according to Bishop Swing, is to

> bring religions and spiritual traditions to a common table,
> where, respecting each other's distinctness, they may seek
> the common ground necessary to make peace among
> themselves and to work together, in dialogue with local,
> national, and international organizations, to create a
> sustainable future for all people on the earth.[10]

To fully realize this grand vision would require substantial funding as well as official backing by the major religions, which has not yet been forthcoming. The process also raises questions about which organizations should be represented, and by whom. Should new religious movements be represented, for instance? Indigenous religions? If so, which ones? If individuals from various faiths were to form such a body, what authority would they have? On the other hand, even if high-ranking officials were to get together with the full backing of their respective communities, would they represent true spiritual vision or only the aims of their own bureaucratic structures? Attempts to develop such bodies continue, even though no definitive resolution of these issues is imminent.

Yet another interfaith process, popular at the turn of the century, is that of trying to define and assert the basic ethical principles that all religions preach. The idea is that the United Nations could adopt and use such a document, as it adopted a Universal Declaration of Human Rights. One of those working to develop such a declaration is Swiss professor Hans Küng. It was his long document, "Moving Toward a Global Ethic," which was discussed and signed provisionally by some of the representatives at the 1993 Chicago Parliament. In essence, his document sets out four basic standards for behavior found in all cultures:

> Do not kill; have respect for all life!
> Do not steal; deal honestly and fairly!
> Do not lie; speak and act truthfully.
> Do not commit sexual immorality; respect and love one another!"[11]

Objections have been raised about Küng's document— that it is too Western, too long, and developed through insufficient interaction with the various religions. Nevertheless, even if such a document were not internationally adopted, it could still serve as a nonsectarian basis for character education of children in schools. Küng's document makes no reference to God, for instance, to avoid alienating people of nontheistic traditions.

Interfaith Worship

In addition to organizational and scholarly attempts to bring greater harmony between people of different religions, our times are witness to attempts to bring them together in worship, too. Interfaith conferences typically include some experiential samples of worship led by people of different faiths. Some interfaith chapels have been built for nonsectarian worship. A number of these are found in international airports, where busy people have time to spare while waiting for delayed flights and might find a quiet religious atmosphere comforting.

Another such initiative is called Universal Worship. Founded by the Sufi mystic Hazrat Inayat Khan early in the twentieth century, it is carried out by ministers who are trained to be knowledgeable about and appreciative of all religions. Scriptures or symbols of the major religions are placed together on an altar, and candles lit for each from a single candle, representing the idea that all are inspired by the same divine light. The ministers lead singing, scriptural readings, and perhaps dancing to give sacred experiences drawn from the various religions. In a single service, the congregants might listen to a reading from the Torah, pray a Christian prayer, chant a Hindu mantra, meditate in Buddhist fashion, and contemplate a flower or stone with sensitivities drawn from indigenous traditions. This contemporary form of worship has had considerable appeal to those who long for spiritual experience rather than institutionalized religion. According to Hazrat Inayat Khan, it is also an expression of the wishes of the prophets in whose name the different religions have been organized:

> This is the fulfillment of the prayer of Moses, the aspiration of Jesus Christ, the desire of Muhammad, the dream of Abraham. They all desired that one day there would come a time when humanity would no longer be divided into different sections.[12]

Another version of this desire is being expressed at a group of spiritual communities in India called Gobind Sadan ("the House of God"). Many who live at the farms and devotional centers run by Gobind Sadan come from the Sikh tradition, which already contains universalist elements (see p. 106). But Hindus, Muslims, Christians, and Jews also live at and visit these places to give volunteer service, to take the spiritual guidance of Gobind Sadan's founder, Baba Virsa Singh, and to celebrate the birthdays of the prophets of various religions. Christmas is typically celebrated with tens of thousands of candles and oil lamps, singing of

At Gobind Sadan, India, members of the community, which encompasses all faiths, are led by the founder, Baba Virsa Singh, and Syrian Orthodox Bishop Paulos Mar Gregorios (foreground) in celebration of Christmas.

festive songs, and a talk by Baba Virsa Singh about the teachings of Jesus. At Gobind Sadan, people honor the birthday of Krishna in Hindu fashion by lovingly pulling a cord to rock an image of him as a baby in a cradle. Celebrations of the birthday of the Prophet Muhammad include ecstatic singing by Muslim *qawalis*, with people of various faiths enthusiastically shouting the refrain, "Prophet Muhammad was born today!"

To encourage his followers to appreciate all religions, Baba Virsa Singh tells them about the lives and teachings of the prophets, rather than the religions institutionalized in their names. He teaches that all the prophets have come from the same one light, which has been given many different names. He explains his point of view:

> I have not adopted any particular religion, because God has given me the feeling that institutionalized religions are fortresses. He said, "I want you to speak about *dharma* [moral order, the essence of religion]. *Dharma* has been created by God. What is *dharma*? Love for everything.
>
> From childhood, I kept questioning God, "In order to love Jesus, must one become a Christian or just love?" He told me, "It is not necessary to become a Christian. It is necessary to love him."
>
> I asked, "To believe in Moses, does one have to observe any special discipline, or just love?" The divine command came, "Only love." I asked, "Does one have to become a Muslim in order to please Muhammad, or only love?" He said, "One must love." "To believe in Buddha, must one become a monk or a Buddhist?" He replied. "No. To believe in Buddha is to love."
>
> Again and again, He said, "I created human beings. Afterward, human beings created sectarian religions. But I created only human beings, not religions."[13]

A Spiritual Future?

Looking across the religious landscape of the planet, we can perceive that it is now alight with activity of all kinds. Although many people regard these as dark days, this is also a very fertile time in spiritual terms. Many religious bodies and individuals are busily engaging themselves with the problems of the material world, and at the same time seeking new ways of reaching toward the ultimate and finding their links with each other. Out of the confusion of rapid modernization and glob-alization are arising many new possiblities and incentives to realize the ancient visions of the prophets of all religions.

Dr. Robert Muller, a leading futurist who was for many years assis-tant secretary-general of the United Nations, describes his vision of the spiritual rebirth which could transform the world:

> At this crucial point of human history, on the eve of the third millennium, the main duty of the religions is not to propagate their dogmas and rituals or to try to increase their memberships. Their main *spiritual* duty is to give the world a desperately needed Renaissance from the extreme materialism and moral decay into which we have fallen. The issue is *not* whether we should pray standing or kneeling, our heads covered or uncovered; it is whether we will pray—period; whether we will be good Samaritans to those in need; whether we can give renewed hope to youth; whether we will revitalize the sacredness of life-giving, belief in the soul, marriage and fidelity. The main duty of religions must be to inspire love for all human brothers and sisters, especially the downtrodden, the poor, the handicapped, abandoned children, the homeless, the refugees, the innocent victims of violence.[14]

Prophets and founders of all religions have tried to show us the way to a better future. Had we truly followed their guidance, perhaps the world would be a very different place than it is now. But the new mil-lennium lies before us, ready to be shaped. In the midst of the post-modern religious ferment, there is room for hope that the twenty-first century will contain many forms of religion which will uplift the human condition.

Notes

1 Global Processses

1. Diana Eck, "A New Geo-Religious Reality," paper presented at the World Conference on Religion and Peace, Sixth World Assembly, Riva del Garda, Italy, November 1994, pp. 4–5.
2. Deepak Chopra, in *Network News*, the newsletter of the Global Network for Spiritual Success, Del Mar, California, January–February 1996.
3. Pope John Paul II, quoted in Joshua Cooper Ramo, "Finding God on the Web," *Time*, December 16, 1996, p. 62.
4. *Bhagavad Gita* 2:71.
5. Pope Paul VI, *Populorum Progressio*, 1967, as quoted in Bishop Labayen, *Alternatives to Consumerism* (Bangkok: Santi Pracha Dhamma Institute, 1997), p. 6.
6. John Kelsay and Sumner B. Twiss (eds), *Religion and Human Rights* (New York: The Project on Religion and Human Rights, 1994), pp. 20–1.
7. Ratikanta Mohanty, "Build Shakti Peeth at Test Site, Says VHP Chief," *Asian Age*, May 19, 1998, p. 4.
8. "Millions in Pak Offer Thanksgiving Prayers," *Asian Age*, May 20, 1998, p. 5.
9. "Humanist Manifesto II," 1973, as reproduced in Joel Beversluis (ed.), *A Sourcebook for Earth's Community of Religions* (Grand Rapids, Michigan: CoNexus Press, 1995), p. 49.
10. Stephen W. Hawking, *A Brief History of Time: From the Big Bang to Black Holes* (London: Bantam Press, 1988).
11. Alain de Benoist, "Confronting Globalization," in *Telos*, no. 108, summer 1996, p. 133.
12. David Ray Griffin, "Introduction: Postmodern Spirituality and Society," in D. R. Griffin (ed.), *Spirituality and Society* (Albany, New York: State University of New York Press, 1988); and "Introduction: Sacred Interconnections," in D. R. Griffin (ed.), *Sacred Interconnection* (Albany, New York; State University of New York Press, 1990).

2 Religious Traditions in the Modern World

1. Chief Seattle's testimony.
2. Black Elk, as quoted in John Neihardt, *Black Elk Speaks* (New York: Pocket Books, 1972), pp. 208–9.
3. Ailton Krenak, in Julian Berger, *The Gaia Atlas of First Peoples* (New York: Doubleday Anchor Books, 1990), p. 167.
4. Margot Adler, "The Juice and the Mystery," in J. Plant (ed.), *Healing the Wounds: The Promise of Ecofeminism* (Philadelphia: New Society Publishers, 1989), p. 151.
5. Starhawk, *The Spiral Dance: A Rebirth of the Ancient Religion of a Great Goddess*, rev. ed. (San Francisco: Harper and Row, 1989), p. 27.
6. Adrian Ivakhiv, "The Resurgence of Magical Religion as a Response to the Crisis of Modernity: A Postmodern Depth Psychological Perspective," in James R. Lewis (ed.), *Magical Religion and Modern Witchcraft* (Albany, New York: State University of New York Press, 1996), p. 242.
7. Ibid., p. 157.
8. Sherrian Lea, quoted in Beth Wolfensberger, "The Return of the Pagans," *Boston Magazine*, May 1992, p. 60.
9. *Chandogya Upanishad, The Upanishads*, trans. by Swami Prabhavananda and Frederick Manchester (New York: Mentor Books, 1957), p. 46.
10. Mirabai, *The Devotional Poems of Mirabai*, trans. by A. J. Alston (Delhi: Motilal Banarsidass, 1980), p. 39.
11. Paramahansa Yogananda, "The Art of Getting Along in this World," reprinted in *Self-realization* magazine, spring 1996, p. 4.

12 Paramahansa Yogananda, *Autobiography of a Yogi*, (Bombay: Jaico Publishing House, 1946; Indian edition 1974), pp. 489–90.

13 Ven. Ajahn Sumedho, *Now is the Knowing*, undated booklet, pp. 21–2.

14 *The Dhammapada*, trans. by P. Lal (162/92 Lake Gardens, Calcutta, 700045, India), p. 152. (Original publishers: New York: Farrar, Straus and Giroux, 1967).

15 Dogen, as quoted in Anne Bancroft, "Women in Buddhism," in Ursula King (ed.), *Women in the World's Religions* (New York: Paragon House, 1987), p. 99.

16 Metta Sutra, as quoted in Fred Eppsteiner (ed.), *The Path of Compassion*, second ed. (Berkeley, California: Parallax Press, 1988), p. xix.

17 Dr. A. T. Ariyaratne, acceptance speech for the Ninth Niwano Peace Prize, in Joel Beversluis (ed.), *A Sourcebook for Earth's Community of Religions*, rev. ed. (Grand Rapids, Michigan: CoNexus Press, 1995), p. 300.

18 Joanna Macy, *Dharma and Development: Religion as Resource in the Sarvodaya Self-Help Movement*, rev. ed. (West Hartford, Connecticut: Kumarian Press, 1985), p. 37.

19 Dr. A. T. Ariyaratne, "Sarvodaya: Self-Help in Sri Lanka," in M. Batchelor and K. Brown (eds), *Buddhism and Ecology*, (London: Cassell, 1992), p. 78.

20 Leviticus 26:12, *Tanakh: The Holy Scriptures* (Philadelphia: Jewish Publication Society, 1988).

21 Deuteronomy 6:4, *Tanakh*, op. cit.

22 Psalm 119:75–7, *Tanakh*, op. cit.

23 See Saul Patai, "A Secular View of Religion in Israel," in Raphael Patai and Emanuel Goldsmith, *Events and Movements in Modern Judaism* (New York: Paragon House, 1995), pp. 183–96.

24 Luke 6:27–33.

25 Matthew 7:14.

26 Matthew 13:41–43.

27 Matthew 13:44.

28 Matthew 15:14.

29 Matthew 28:18–20.

30 World Council of Churches, "Baptism, Eucharist and Ministry," Faith and Order Paper No. 111, Geneva, 1982, p. 2.

31 Acts 2:2–4.

32 Joel 2:28.

33 Charles Harrison Mason, as quoted in Joe Maxwell, "Building the Church (of God in Christ)," *Christianity Today*, April 8, 1996, vol. 40:4, p. 22.

34 Bishop Ithiel Clemmons, as quoted in Joe Maxwell, *Christianity Today*, op. cit., p. 28.

35 Sura 98:5, *The Qur'an*, adapted by M. A. Haleem Eliasii from English translations by Mohammad Marmaduke Pickthall, as reprinted in *The Qur'an: Transliteration in Roman Script*, rev. ed. (Delhi: Jama Masjid, Madeena Company, 1990); and Abdullah Yusuf Ali, as amended in *The Qur'an:, English Translation of the Meanings and Commentary*, revised and edited by the Presidency of Islamic Researches, Ifta, Call and Guidance (Medina: King Fahd Holy Qur'an Printing Complex, no date).

36 Sura 3:79, *The Qur'an*.

3 New Religious Movements

1 Timothy Miller, personal communication, May 9, 1998.

2 Max Weber, *The Theory of Social and Economic Organization*, trans. by A. M. Henderson and T. Parsons (New York: Free Press, 1947), p. 358.

3 Tamal Krishna Goswami, "Servant of the Servant: A. C. Bhaktivedanta Swami Prabhupada, Founder-acharya of the International Society for Krishna Consciousness," paper given at the Inter-Religious Federation for World Peace conference, "The Founders and Shapers of the World's Religions," November 25–29, 1997, Washington, D.C., p. 5.

4 Keith Ward, *Religion and Revelation* (Oxford: Oxford University Press, 1994), p. 89.

5 "Testimony of the Prophet Joseph Smith," *The Book of Mormon: Another Testament of*

Jesus Christ (Salt Lake City, Utah: The Church of Jesus Christ of Latter-Day Saints, 1830, in 1981 ed.), unpaginated introduction.

6   "The Testimony of Eight Witnesses," *The Book of Mormon*, op. cit., unpaginated text.

7   2 Nephi 29:10, *The Book of Mormon*, op. cit., p. 110.

8   The Book of Mormon 8:28–33, *The Book of Mormon*, op. cit.

9   Marianne Williamson, *Illuminata: A Return to Prayer* (New York: Riverhead Books, 1994), pp. 4–6, 17–19.

10   Mark 13: 7–8, 19.

11   Mircea Eliade, *The Sacred and the Profane: The Nature of Religion*, trans. by Willard R. Trask (New York: Harcourt, Brace and World, 1957), p. 92.

12   Christina and Stanislov Grof, *The Stormy Search for the Self: A Guide to Personal Growth through Transformational Crisis* (New York: Perigee-Tarcher-Putnam, 1992).

13   Dr. Marc Galanter, quoted in Daniel Coleman, "A Cultist's Mind," *New York Times*, April 21, 1993, p. 177.

14   Dean Kelley, in Charles S. Clark, "Cults in America," *Congressional Quarterly Researcher*, vol. 3, no. 17, May 7, 1993, pp. 387+.

15   Reverend Sun Myung Moon, "The Healing of the World: An Introduction to the Life and Teachings of Sun Myung Moon," in *Unification Movement*, p. 19.

16   See Michael L. Mickler, "Charismatic Leadership Trajectories: Two Case Histories," in Jeffrey K. Hadden and Anson Shupe (eds), *Prophetic Religions and Politics*, (New York: Paragon House, 1986).

17   Reverend Sun Myung Moon, "In Search of the Origin of the Universe," founder's address, Inauguration of the Family Federation for World Peace in 185 Nations, as delivered November 6, 1996, New Delhi, India, p. 22.

18   Jacob K. Olupona, "Samuel Bileou Oschoffa and the Story of the Celestial Church of Christ in West Africa," paper presented at Inter-Religious Federation for World Peace conference, Washington D.C., November 1997.

19   Samuel Oschoffa, as interviewed by Funmilola Olorunisola, *Drum Magazine*, January 1989, p. 6.

4 Relationships Between Religions

1   See Matthew 8:18–22; John 3 to 10.

2   Buddha, *The Dhammapada*, trans. by P .Lal (162/92 Lake Gardens, Calcutta, 700045, India), p. 152.

3   W.T. Stace, *Mysticism and Philosophy* (New York: J.B. Lippincott Company, 1960), p. 297.

4   Guru Nanak, as quoted in W. Owen Cole and Piara Singh Sambhi, *The Sikhs: Their Religious Beliefs and Practices* (London: Routledge and Kegan Paul, 1978), p. 39.

5   Guru Gobind Singh, "*Manas ki jaat*," Dasam Granth, compiled by Bhai Mani Singh Shaheed, 1721, Amritsar, India; Chattar Singh/Jiwan Singh publishers, p. 19.

6   Baha'u'llah, as quoted in booklet, *The Baha'is: A Profile of the Baha'i Faith and its Worldwide Community*, (Leicestershire, UK: Baha'i Publishing Trust, 1992), p. 50.

7   Fariburz Sahba, in souvenir book, *The Dawning Place of Remembrance of God*, issued by Baha'i Temple Project of the National Spiritual Assembly of the Baha'is of India, p. 11.

8   Swami Vivekananda, speech for the Parliament of the World's Religions, Chicago, 1893.

9   Brother Wayne Teasdale, "Sacred Community at the Dawn of the Second Axial Age," in Beversluis, op. cit., p. 100

10   The Rt. Rev. William E. Swing, "United Religions Initiative 2000: An Invitation to Share the Vision, An Invitation to Change the World," July 1996. Pub details?

11   Dr. Daniel Gomez-Ibanez, "Moving Toward a Global Ethic," in Beversluis, op. cit., p. 127.

12   Hazrat Inayat Khan, "A New Form," in *Addresses to Cherags* (Lebanon Springs, New York: Sufi Order), p. 75.

13   Baba Virsa Singh, remarks to J. Hollister, "News from Gobind Sadan," August 1997, p. 1.

14   Robert Muller, "Preparing for the Next Millennium," in Beversluis, op. cit., p. 4

Glossary

Allah	In Islam, the Name of God, which encompasses all divine attributes.
Anti-christ	In some Christians' belief, a hypothesized arch-enemy of Christ who will appear when the world is about to end.
anti-cult network	A group of organizations attempting to suppress new religious movements, considering them dangerous.
apocalypse	A dramatic end to the present world, as anticipated by some religions.
ashram	A spiritual community of people centered on a guru.
atheist	A person who believes that there is no supernatural power.
atma	In Hindu belief, the eternal soul, which continues through many reincarnations.
Axial Age	A period between roughly the eighth to fifth centuries B.C.E. when many great religious leaders appeared, including Buddha, Confucius, Jewish prophets, and certain Greek philosophers.
baptism	Sacred purification of sins by water, and, in Christianity, admission into the Church.
bhakti	In Indian religions, the way of intense devotion to one's most beloved manifestation of the divine.
Boddhi-satva	In Buddhism, one who devotes his or her life to becoming enlightened and saving others from suffering.
Brahman	In Hindu belief, the divine source of everything.
charisma	The magnetic attraction of a spiritual leader.
Christ	Greek word meaning "messiah," applied to Jesus.
covenant	A sacred commitment, as of God with the Israelites.
creed	Formal affirmation of the beliefs of a particular religion.
criminali-zation	In this context, labeling of controversial new religious movements as illegal.
crisis of modernity	The social and psychological disruption which has accompanied modernization.
cult	A religious movement devoted to a particular person or deity.
depro-gramming	Controversial techniques to forcibly separate people from new religious movements.
dharma	In Indian religions, moral order in the universe, expressed as righteousness in human affairs. Buddhists also refer to the teachings of the Buddha as the Dharma.
diaspora	Members of a religion living away from their religion's original geographical base.
dramati-zation	Overt attempts by controversial new religious movements to publicize and carry out their special mission.
ecumenism	Unity among Christian churches, or, more broadly, among all religions.
enlighten-ment	Inner realization of the ultimate reality.
Eucharist	In Christianity, **sacramental** sharing of bread and wine or grape juice in order to become part of the "body" of Christ.
evangelism	Especially in Christianity, public attempts to spread the faith and make

converts.

exclusivism The belief that only one's own group and one's own prophet are correct, and all others are outside the truth.

feminist theology Interpretation of religion favoring women's inclusion and power.

fundamenta- lism The drive to adhere to what are regarded as the traditional ways of a religion, in contrast to modern liberalization.

global village The geographically expanded community of people who forge links with each other across great distances via modern computer and satellite systems.

globalization The contemporary linking of cultures around the globe by financial, transportation, and communication systems.

gospel In Christianity, the "good news" about Jesus contained in the first four books of the New Testament of the Bible.

gurdwara Sikh temple.

guru In Indian religions, one's living spiritual master.

hajj In Islam, sacred pilgrimage to Mecca at a particular time of year.

holocaust The murder of some six million Jews by Nazi Germany during the Second World War.

humanism The belief that it is up to humans rather than some transcendent deity actively to work for people's salvation.

inclusivism The idea that all faiths can fit under the roof of one broad religion (preferably one's own).

indigenous spirituality The faithways practiced by members of small-scale cultures who still occupy their ancient land and are relatively unaffected by modern industrial society.

interfaith Referring to positive relationships between religions.

karma In Indian religions, the shaping of our future lives by our good or bad deeds.

liberation theology In Christianity, an interpretation of the faith which emphasizes direct social action on behalf of the poor.

magic Shaping events by working with supernatural forces.

Mahayana One of the major divisions of Buddhism, comprising a variety of belief-systems, which evolved in east Asia.

messiah Deliverer of the people, as anticipated by the Jews, or as recognized by Christians in the form of Jesus.

millennium In Christianity, the anticipated coming of a 1000-year golden age.

moderni- zation Major social transformations stemming from industrialization and urbanization.

monotheism Belief in a singular supreme divine power.

multicultural encompassing lifeways from different parts of the world.

Neo-pagan A contemporary practitioner of nature-oriented modes of spirituality derived from ancient beliefs, but given modern expression in forms such as Wicca or Goddess Spirituality.

networking Widening the scope of one's work or mission through a web of contacts between individuals or organizations.

nirvana The ultimate bliss of spiritual realization and relinquishing of the ego.

Noachide laws The spiritual commandments which Jews believe were originally given to Adam and Noah by God.

nontheistic Referring to religions which do not mention any personal deity but may instead, like Buddhism, allude to eternal cosmic principles.

pagan A negative label historically applied to people who were not Jewish,

	Christian, or Muslim.
parable	A simple story illustrating a moral or religious lesson.
Pentecost	An event after the death and resurrection of Jesus, in which his disciples experienced the spirit of God being showered upon them like fire from above.
pluralism	Simultaneous coexistence of different peoples, or religions, in one geographical location.
polytheism	Worship of many deities.
postmodern	Referring to late twentieth-century reactions to modernization.
postmodern spirituality	A constellation of modern religious beliefs not linked to any particular religion but which includes reverence for nature, equality for the sexes, and belief that the divine and human beings together create reality.
quantum physics	Study of the smallest particles of matter.
Qur'an	The holy scripture of Islam, revealed to the Prophet Muhammad.
rabbi	A Jewish teacher or leader of a congregation.
reincarnation	Rebirth of the individual soul after death of its previous physical body.
routinization of charisma	Translation of a religious leader's spiritual appeal into an organizational structure.
sacrament	In Christianity, a ritual which is the outer expression of the inner bestowal of grace.
samadhi	In Hinduism, spiritual absorption into the all-pervading divine presence.
Sanatana Dharma	The technically correct term for what is more commonly called "Hinduism."
sect	A splinter group or subgroup of a larger religion.
self-stigmatization	New religious movements' adoptions of an openly controversial identity.
shaman	A man or woman who is thought to have special visionary powers to communicate with the spirit world and to draw from there methods of healing.
shariah	Islamic law, based on interpretations of the Qur'an and stories from the life of the Prophet Muhammad.
soft religion	De-emphasis on boundaries between religion in favor of similar spiritual experiences across religions.
syncretism	The process by which two or more religions become fused to form a new religion.
textual criticism	Objective, rather than faith-based, study of sacred scriptures.
theistic	Referring to religions based on belief in a supreme deity or deities.
Theravada	One of the major divisions of Buddhism, comprising what are considered to be the earlier traditions.
Torah	The Jewish Bible, or its teachings.
Vedas	Ancient divinely inspired literature of India, the scriptural basis of what is now called "Hinduism."
yoga	An ancient Indian practice that aids union with the ultimate reality.
zaddik	In Judaism, a charismatic Hasidic teacher.

Pronunciation Guide

This guide gives an accepted pronunciation as simply as possible. Syllables are separated by a space and those that are stressed are printed in italics. Letters are pronounced in the usual manner for English unless they are clarified in the following list.

a	fl*a*t	ihr	*ea*r
ah	f*a*ther	ō	n*o*
ai	th*e*re	o	n*o*t
aw	s*aw*	oo	f*oo*d
ay	p*ay*	ow	h*ow*
ee	s*ee*	u	b*u*t
e	l*e*t	ă	*a*bout
ī	h*i*gh	izm	triba*lism*
i	p*i*ty	j	*j*et

agnostic: ag *nos* tik	hajj: hahj
Allah: *ahl lah*	karma: *kahr* mă
apocalypse: ă *pah* kă lips	Mahayana: mah hah *yah* nah
ashram: *ahsh* răm	nirvana: nihr *vah* nă
atheist: *ay* thee ist	Qur'an: kōr *an*
atma: *aht* mă	rabbi: *ra* bī
bhakti: *bahk* tee	samadhi: să *mah* dee
bhikkuni: *bik* oo nee	Sanatana dharma: sah *nah* tah nah
Boddhisatva: bō dee *saht* vah	*dahr* mă
charisma: kar *iz* mă	sura: *soo* ră
dharma: *dahr* ma	syncretism: *sing* krăt izm
ecumenism: ek *yoo* men izm	Theravada: thai ră *vah* dă
Eucharist: *yoo* kă rist	Torah: *tō* rah
gurdwara: *goor* dwah ră	Vedas: *vay* dăz
guru: *goo* roo	zaddik: *zah* dik

Suggested Further Reading

Chapter 1

HAROLD COWARD, *Sacred Word and Sacred Text: Scripture in World Religions* (Maryknoll, New York: Orbis Books, 1988)
A helpful analysis of both faithful and scholarly approaches to the scriptures of major religions.

KITTY FERGUSON, *The Fire in the Equations: Science, Religion and the Search for God* (New York: Bantam Books, 1994)
A highly readable and interesting survey of contemporary science and the dialogue now opening up between science and religion.

JOHN KELSAY and SUMNER B. TWISS, *Religion and Human Rights* (New York: The Project on Religion and Human Rights, 1994)
Relevant scholarship on militant "fundamentalism."

URSULA KING, *Women and Spirituality: Voices of Protest and Promise*, 2nd edn (University Park, Pennsylvania: The Pennsylvania State University Press, 1993)
A survey of the many ways in which feminism is affecting religion.

WILLIAM E. PADEN, *Interpreting the Sacred: Ways of Viewing Religion* (Boston: Beacon Press, 1992)
A gentle journey through perspectives on the study of religion.

NINIAN SMART, *The World's Religions*, 2nd edn (Cambridge, UK: Cambridge University Press, 1998)
Religions understood through world history, and as constantly developing systems of belief.

Chapter 2

JULIAN BURGER, *The Gaia Atlas of First Peoples: A Future for the Indigenous World* (New York: Doubleday Anchor Books, 1990)
A global survey of the efforts of indigenous peoples to protect their fragile rights and environments.

HARVEY COX, *Fire From Heaven: The Rise of Pentecostal Spirituality and the Reshaping of Religion in the Twenty-first Century* (Reading, Massachusetts: Addison-Wesley Publishing Company, 1995)
A major Christian theologian describes the importance of the Pentecostal movement.

FRED EPPSTEINER (ed.), *The Path of Compassion: Writings on Socially Engaged Buddhism* (Berkeley, California: Parallax Press, 1988)
Leading Buddhists describe specific ways in which practitioners of the religion are becoming deeply involved in alleviating social problems.

MARY PAT FISHER, *Living Religions*, 3rd edn (Upper Saddle River, New Jersey: Prentice Hall, 1997)
An appreciative inside look at the world's religions, with particular emphasis on how they are practiced today.

YVONNE YAZBECK HADDAD (ed.), *The Muslims of America* (New York and Oxford: Oxford University Press, 1991)
Muslim and non-Muslim scholars discuss the relationships between Islam and American society.

SUSANNAH HESCHEL (ed.), *On Being a Jewish Feminist* (New York: Schocken Books, 1995)
A collection of writings exploring ways of being both a feminist and an observant Jew.

JAMES R. LEWIS (ed.), *Magical Religion and Modern Witchcraft* (Albany, New York: State

University of New York Press, 1996)
Accounts of Neo-paganism by practitioner-scholars.

SEYYED HOSSEIN NASR, *Traditional Islam in the Modern World* (London and New York: Kegan Paul International, 1987)
A major Muslim scholar surveys the responses of Islam to modernization.

JACOB K. OLUPONA (ed.), *African Traditional Religions in Contemporary Society* (New York: Paragon House, 1991)
Insightful essays on African traditions as they are practiced in today's social contexts.

MADHURI SANTANAM SONDHI, *Modernity, Morality and the Mahatma* (New Delhi: Har-Anand Publications, 1997)
Brilliant study of the impacts of modernization on traditional Indian religious ways.

Chapter 3

MIGENE GONZALEZ-WIPPLER, *Santeria: The Religion*, 2nd edn (St. Paul, Minnesota: Llewellyn Publications, 1996)
An anthropologist and Santeria initiate describes the usually hidden ways of this syncretistic faith.

JEFFREY K. HADDEN and ANSON SHUPE (eds), *Prophetic Religions and Politics: Religion and the Political Order* (New York: Paragon House, 1986)
Extremist, charismatic, and millennial groups' involvements with politics.

TIMOTHY MILLER (ed.), *America's Alternative Religions* (Albany, New York: State University of New York Press, 1995)
Forty-three case studies of new religious movements.

TIMOTHY MILLER (ed.), *When Prophets Die: The Postcharismatic Fate of New Religious Movements* (Albany, New York: State University of New York Press, 1991)
Interesting case studies of the processes by which new religions have perpetuated themselves or declined.

Chapter 4

JOEL BEVERSLUIS (ed.), *A Sourcebook for Earth's Community of Religions*, rev. edn (Grand Rapids, Michigan: CoNexus Press, 1995)
Like the Chicago Parliament of the World's Religions, for which it was originally written, this provides a diverse sample of short articles on old and new religions with reference to today's social issues.

MARCUS BRAYBROOKE, *Faith and Interfaith in a Global Age* (Grand Rapids, Michigan: CoNexus Press, 1998)
One of the world's foremost organizers of interfaith dialogue personally surveys all aspects of the movement.

WILLIAM CENKNER (ed.), *Evil and the Response of World Religion* (St. Paul, Minnesota: Paragon House, 1997)
Interesting discussions of the ways in which many religions have explained the existence of evil and suffering in the world.

MARTIN FORWARD (ed.), *Ultimate Visions: Reflections on the Religions We Choose* (Oxford, UK: Oneworld Publishing, 1995)
Interesting personal essays by leading scholars and theologians about why they prefer their religion over others, presented in a context of interfaith appreciation.

LARRY D. SHIN (ed.), *God: In Search of the Divine: Some Unexpected Consequences of Interfaith Dialogue* (New York: Paragon House, 1987)
Scholars of various religions compare their concepts of ultimate reality.

KEITH WARD, *Religion and Revelation* (Oxford: Clarendon Press, 1994)
A leading Christian theologian looks at the concept of revelation from an interfaith perspective, in Christianity, Judaism, Islam, Hinduism, and Buddhism.

Index